SUTTON POCKET HISTORIES

THE
VIKINGS

JOHN HAYWOOD

Happy Reading to a
future writer · - - - -

Lots of love,

SUTTON PUBLISHING

Mum.

11 - 02 - 2001.

First published in the United Kingdom in 1999 by
Sutton Publishing Limited · Phoenix Mill
Thrupp · Stroud · Gloucestershire · GL5 2BU

British Library Cataloguing in Publication Data
A catalogue record for this book is available from the British
Library.

ISBN 0-7509-2194-3

Cover picture: *Life, Passion and Miracles of St Edmund (c. 1130);
M. 736 f. 9v Invasion of Danes under Hinguar (Ingvar) and Hubba,
made at Bury St Edmunds in England (manuscript). (The Pierpont
Morgan Library/Art Resource, New York)*

 ALAN SUTTON™ and SUTTON™ are the
trade marks of Sutton Publishing Limited

Typeset in 11/14.5 pt Baskerville.
Typesetting and origination by
Sutton Publishing Limited.
Printed in Great Britain by
The Guernsey Press Company Limited,
Guernsey, Channel Islands.

Contents

To Jack, for letting me stay up late to watch The Vikings

List of Dates

834–7	Dorestad on the Rhine is raided annually.
841	Viking base is established at Dublin.
843	Treaty of Verdun partitions the Carolingian empire.
844	Viking army in Spain is defeated at Seville.
845	The Danes sack Hamburg and Paris.
859–62	Hastein and Bjorn Ironside raid in the Mediterranean.
c. 860	Gardar the Swede explores the coast of Iceland.
860	The first Rus attack on Constantinople is driven off.
c. 862	Rurik becomes ruler of Novgorod; Askold and Dyr seize Kiev.
865	Danish 'Great Army' invades England.
c. 870–930	The Vikings settle Iceland.
c. 870	The earldom of Orkney is established by Rognvald of Møre.
876–9	The beginning of Danish settlement in eastern England.
878	Alfred the Great of Wessex defeats the Danes at Edington, Wiltshire.
c. 882	Oleg unites Novgorod and Kiev.
c. 885–90	Harald Finehair wins the battle of Hafrsfjord, uniting most of Norway.
885–6	Viking siege of Paris is defeated.
c. 900	Norwegian settlement begins in north-west England.
902	Irish expel the Vikings from Dublin.
907	After a failed attack on Constantinople the Rus agree a trade treaty with the Byzantine empire.

911	Viking leader Rollo is made count of Rouen, founding Normandy.
912–54	Wessex conquers the Danelaw.
914–36	Vikings occupy Brittany.
917	Vikings under Sihtric Cáech recapture Dublin.
c. **930**	Foundation of the Icelandic Althing.
937	English defeat a Scottish-Norse alliance at Brunanburh.
954	Erik Bloodaxe, last Viking king of York, is killed at Stainmore.
964–71	Svyatoslav of Kiev campaigns against the Bulgars, Khazars and Byzantines.
965	Harald Bluetooth of Denmark is converted to Christianity.
c. **965**	Exhaustion of Muslim silver mines leads to the decline of Viking trade routes to the east.
986	Erik the Red leads the Norse settlement of Greenland.
988	Byzantine emperor Basil II founds the Varangian Guard. Vladimir prince of Kiev converts to Orthodox Christianity.
991	Olaf Tryggvason defeats the English at Maldon.
995	Olaf Tryggvason wins control of Norway; adopts a policy of forcible Christianization. Olof Skötkonung becomes the first king to rule both the Svear and Götar.
1000	Olaf Tryggvason is killed at the battle of Svöld. The Icelanders accept Christianity.

c. 1000	Voyages to Vinland begin.
1013	Svein Forkbeard of Denmark conquers England.
1014	Brian Boru, High King of Ireland, defeats Norse-Leinster alliance at Clontarf.
1015	Olaf Haraldsson (St Olaf) becomes King of Norway.
1016	Cnut becomes King of England.
1030	Olaf Haraldsson killed at the battle of Stiklestad.
1042	End of Danish rule in England.
1066	Harald Hardrada killed at the battle of Stamford Bridge.
1075	Last Danish invasion of England.
1086	Cnut II of Denmark is murdered after abandoning a planned invasion of England.
1098	Magnus Barelegs establishes Norwegian royal authority in the Scottish isles.
1107–11	Norwegian King Sigurd Jorsalafari leads an expedition to the Holy Land.

Map 1: The Vinland Voyages.

a Ladoga

CIPALITY OF
KIEV

BULGARS

Kiev

PECHENEGS

KHAZARS

Constantinople

EMPIRE

ABBASID   CALIPHATE

Baghdad

Map 2: The Viking
World, *c.* 900.

ONE

Origins

One day in or around 789 Beaduheard, a reeve of the king of Wessex, rode to the small Channel port of Portland to meet what he believed were three merchant ships recently arrived from Norway. Beaduheard intended to order the visitors to attend the royal manor at nearby Dorchester: instead he achieved the dubious distinction of becoming the first person known to have been killed in the course of a Viking raid. For the next three hundred years, the Vikings would play a central role in the history of Europe. In Britain the Vikings broke up existing power structures, paving the way for the creation of the unified kingdoms of England and Scotland. In Ireland they founded the first towns. On the Continent they hastened, though did not directly cause, the break-up of the mighty Carolingian empire and founded the principality of Normandy, which was to have a decisive influence on the subsequent history of France, England and Italy. In eastern Europe it was the Vikings who founded the first Russian state. The Vikings were the first settlers of Iceland and the first Europeans to reach Greenland and North America. The influence in turn of the rest of Europe on the Vikings was even greater. As a result of contact with their neighbours, the Vikings were themselves transformed from pagan barbarians into Christian Europeans by 1100. To understand this dramatic movement, it is first necessary to know something of Scandinavia's geography and prehistory.

The homeland of the Vikings was made up of the three modern Scandinavian countries of Denmark, Norway and Sweden. Scandinavia is a vast region, stretching from the neck of the Jutland peninsula in the south to North Cape, over 500 kilometres north of the Arctic Circle. Only at its north-eastern and southern extremities does Scandinavia lack clearly defined borders. In the north-east, Scandinavia merges into the vast tundra of northern Russia. Still sparsely populated today, in Viking times this region was inhabited by Lapp hunter-gatherers who ranged as far south as central Sweden and Norway. Scandinavia's short southern land border across the

neck of the Jutland peninsula has always been hard
to define. Its present position dates only to 1920 and
in Viking times Danish settlement extended to the
River Eider in the modern German province of
Schleswig-Holstein. Southern Jutland has extensive
areas of infertile sandy soils, so until the
introduction of modern farming methods it
remained a thinly populated area forming a natural
buffer zone between the Germans to the south and
the Scandinavians to the north.

Southern Scandinavia, that is Jutland, the Danish
islands and the modern Swedish provinces of
Blekinge, Halland and Skåne, is a low lying
extension of the north European plain. Despite
large areas of infertile sands and gravels laid down
by rivers of meltwater from ice sheets at the end of
the last Ice Age, this region has the best soils in
Scandinavia. North of Blekinge and Halland lie the
Swedish Southern Uplands, an area of lakes, bogs,
dense forest and rocky outcrops which were a
significant obstacle to travel and formed the border
between the Danes and Swedes until the
seventeenth century. This was therefore the Danes'
'march' or border for which Denmark is named.
Norway on the west side of the Scandinavian

peninsula is dominated by the long range of ancient fold mountains known as The Keel. These rise steeply from the Atlantic and decline gradually in the east and south to the Gulf of Bothnia and the lowlands around Lake Mälaren and Lake Vänern in central Sweden. Norway's coast is deeply indented by fjords, several of which penetrate over 100 kilometres inland. Offshore are chains of islands and reefs, the Skerry Guard, which provides a sheltered passage for coastal shipping. This sea route to the north, the North Way, has given Norway its name. The Scandinavian peninsula was subject to heavy glaciation during the last Ice Age and, except in the far south, the landscape has been scoured by ice. As a result soils are generally thin, full of stones, waterlogged and infertile. Only around Trondheim and Oslo Fjord in Norway and around Lakes Mälaren and Vänern in Sweden are there extensive areas of fertile soils.

Despite its northerly latitude – even Denmark is as far north as Labrador, where permafrost makes agriculture almost impossible – Scandinavia has a remarkably mild climate, thanks to the warming influence of the Atlantic Gulf Stream. The Norwegian coast has a high rainfall, cool summers and mild winters: the sea remains ice free. Though it is a poor climate for growing grain it supports good pasture, making farming based on stock rearing possible even in the Lofoten Islands, 200 kilometres north of the Arctic Circle. The climate deteriorates rapidly with altitude but the mountains were important in Viking times for summer grazing and as a source of bog-iron ore. Lying in the rain shadow of The Keel, Sweden has warm sunny summers, but being isolated from the influence of the Gulf Stream it also has severe winters and the Baltic Sea can freeze for several weeks or even months a year. The climate of Denmark and the far south of Sweden is a mixture of maritime and continental influences with a moderate rainfall, warm summers and cold but rarely severe winters. This climate is well suited to both pastoral and arable farming which, combined with the region's good soils, has always made Denmark and southern Sweden Scandinavia's richest farming area.

The geography and environment of Scandinavia have always had an important influence on its history. Mountains, forests and bogs were major obstacles to communications in the Scandinavian peninsula until modern times: as a result, most long-distance overland travel took place in winter when the ground was frozen hard. In contrast, Scandinavia is well provided with sheltered coastal waters, fjords, lakes and navigable rivers. From the Stone Age onwards, boats and ships were the most important means of transport: the Vikings were heirs to a long tradition of shipbuilding and seafaring. The poverty of the land in so much of Scandinavia was another incentive to the development of a seafaring tradition. Fishing, sealing, walrus hunting and trade were all attractive ways to supplement a hard living by farming. The shortage of good farmland may also have bred a willingness to emigrate overseas in times of population growth. The environment too profoundly affected Scandinavia's political development. As the Danes controlled most of Scandinavia's good arable land, they were the wealthiest and most numerous of the Scandinavian peoples in the Viking age. Communications by both sea and land were also easiest in Denmark and the Danish settled area of southern Sweden so it is not surprising that it was the first area of Scandinavia to see the emergence of a centralized kingdom in the Viking age. It also explains why Denmark, despite its small size, remained Scandinavia's most powerful kingdom until the seventeenth century. In contrast, the rugged geography of Norway lent itself to the formation of strong local identities. The only two large areas of good farmland, around Trondheim and Oslo Fjord, and therefore the most densely settled and wealthiest parts of the country, were widely separated. They therefore developed as rival power centres, delaying the unification of the country. Central Sweden also had strong local identities in the Viking age, based on its main areas of good farmland. To the north, in the Lake Mälaren lowlands, was the power centre of the Svear, the people for whom Sweden (*Sverige*) is named. To the south, around Lakes Vänern and Vättern were the Götar. Though the Svear were already the stronger of the two peoples at the beginning of the Viking age, they were not securely united until the twelfth century. Geography also determined the main areas of activity of the Scandinavian peoples: the Viking movement east was dominated by the Swedes, while the main areas of Danish Viking activity were Frisia, the Low Countries, the Seine and Loire valleys and south-eastern England. Scotland, Ireland and north-west England were the main areas of Norwegian activity.

7

The first human inhabitants of Scandinavia arrived around 11000 BC, towards the end of the last Ice Age. They were nomadic hunters, following the seasonal migrations of herds of reindeer across what was then the north German tundra. With the end of the Ice Age around 8000 BC, bands of hunter-gatherers began to settle permanently in southern Scandinavia, gradually spreading further north as the climate ameliorated. There is no evidence that there has ever been any significant subsequent migration into Scandinavia so it is probable that the Vikings were the descendants of these original post-Ice Age settlers (as, indeed, are modern Scandinavians). These hunter-gatherer bands moved between seasonal camps to exploit a wide range of animal and plant foods. Especially in the south, there was a wide range of marine, freshwater and terrestrial habitats and food was plentiful. The population rose slowly but steadily, eventually outstripping the environment's capacity to feed it. By about 4000 BC these early Scandinavians had adopted farming, probably as a result of contact with the Neolithic peoples of northern Germany. Around 2000 BC bronze tools began to replace those of flint and by about 500 BC the first iron tools had come into use.

The Scandinavian Neolithic farmers lived in isolated family farms and buried their dead in impressive communal megalithic tombs. In the Bronze Age, farms began to cluster in small villages in the more fertile areas, though in most of Norway and central Sweden, dispersed settlement remained the norm until the end of the Viking age. The presence of a single larger dwelling among otherwise smaller dwellings indicates that villages were dominated by a single headman or chief. Small numbers of graves with rich burial offerings also point to the emergence of a social elite in Bronze Age Scandinavia. This process of increasing social stratification and centralization of power continued throughout the Scandinavian Iron Age (*c.* 500 BC–AD 800) culminating in the emergence of centralized kingdoms at the end of the Viking age.

The beginning of the Scandinavian Early Iron Age (500 BC–AD 1) was marked by a decline in population, possibly the result of a climatic deterioration, but by its end the population had begun to increase again and it continued to do so right up until the Black Death in the fourteenth century. Characteristic of this period are votive offerings of weapons, cauldrons, pottery, food and human sacrificial victims deposited in bogs and often superbly preserved by the acid conditions. In the Roman Iron Age (AD 1–400) and the following Germanic Iron Age (400–800), Scandinavian society began to assume its Viking characteristics. There are few contemporary literary sources for this period and it is impossible at this distance in time to be sure how much faith to place in the legendary historical traditions recorded by medieval Scandinavian writers such as Saxo Grammaticus and Snorri Sturluson. Because of this it is impossible to reconstruct the history of the period in any detail, but the main political and social changes can be determined from archaeological evidence and by comparison with the better documented Germanic peoples to the south.

Archaeological evidence indicates that in the Roman Iron Age war came to play an increasingly important role in Scandinavian society. Votive deposits in bogs consist almost exclusively of weapons: presumably thank-offerings to the gods for victory in battle. In Denmark in particular, many of these weapons were of Roman origin, suggesting that the Scandinavians often fought their German neighbours, who were in direct contact with the

Roman Empire. The appearance of graves richly furnished with weapons indicates that Scandinavian society was now dominated by a warrior elite. A small number of graves, equipped not only with weapons but also imported luxury goods, suggests that there existed a class of chieftains or even petty kings. Finds of Roman coins, pottery, glass, silverware and jewellery point to trade contacts (direct or indirect) with the Roman Empire and seasonal trading centres sprang up. Many of these, such as Lundeborg on the Danish island of Fyn, were associated with pagan cult centres. A concentration of Roman imports on the Danish island of Sjælland in the late Roman Iron Age suggests that a kingdom had developed here with sufficient power to control trade over a wide area.

These far-reaching social changes in Scandinavia were probably caused indirectly by the influence of the Roman Empire on the Germanic tribes to the south. The Germanic tribes along the Empire's northern border became enriched through a combination of trade, subsidy, plundering raids and wages paid to mercenary soldiers. This made them attractive targets for raiding by their poorer and no doubt envious northern neighbours: some tribes even migrated south, jostling other tribes aside as they tried to establish themselves on the Roman border. Those who were most successful in these conflicts would soon have been set apart from the rest of society by their greater wealth and status. This period probably saw the development of the *comitatus* or war band in Scandinavia, an institution which is well documented among the Germanic peoples. The *comitatus* was the warrior retinue of a chieftain or king (known as the *lið* in Viking Scandinavia). In return for their loyalty and service the warriors expected to be rewarded and the *comitatus* would only stay together for as long as its leader had the means to do this. Though a chieftain or king could gain wealth by control of land and trade, military expeditions to win plunder or payments of tribute were far more effective. This led to the development of what was a violent, predatory and very competitive society in which success at war was the key to power and status. It also accelerated the tendency, begun in the Bronze Age, for power to be concentrated in fewer and fewer hands. Another result was the merging of tribes, either voluntarily so as to wage war more effectively or by the conquest of weaker tribes by stronger. It was probably in this way

12

that the Danes, for example, became the dominant people of southern Scandinavia in the sixth century.

In the early Germanic Iron Age or Migration Period (400–550), Scandinavian society became even more intensely competitive and warlike. Fortifications proliferated – over 1,500 are known with particularly dense concentrations in southern Norway, western and central Sweden and the Baltic islands of Öland and Gotland. Scandinavia suffered no invasions from outside in this period so these can only be seen as signs of insecurity born of intense internal power struggles. It may be that the Jutes and Angles, both from Jutland, who joined the Saxons in their migrations to Britain in the fifth century, did so because they were under pressure from neighbouring peoples. There was also a marked tendency for settlement to move away from the coasts, a clear sign that piracy was rife. On Fyn, for example, a zone 3–4 kilometres deep around the island's entire coast became completely depopulated. Not until the later Middle Ages was this area resettled. Though they cannot be regarded as reliable historical accounts, Scandinavia's legendary historical traditions also hold that this was a period marked by frequent conflicts between competing peoples.

In the late Germanic Iron Age (550–800), the last period of Scandinavian prehistory before the Viking age, powerful regional kingdoms began to develop. The most impressive evidence of this comes from Denmark where, in 726, a canal was built through an isthmus on the island of Samsø, presumably to regulate shipping passing through the Great Belt straits which lead into the Baltic Sea, and in 737 an earthwork barrier, known as the Danevirke, was built across the neck of the Jutland peninsula. (We have such exact details because the timbers used in these constructions have been dated precisely by dendrochronology, the technique of dating by studying the pattern of annual growth rings in timber.) These were both major building projects and whoever was responsible for them must have been able to command the labour and resources of a wide area. Around 710 a trading place was founded at Ribe on the North Sea coast. As it was divided up neatly into rectangular plots, this too must have been done under some form of central direction. It is possible that all these works were the responsibility of King Angantyr, who the Anglo-Saxon missionary St Willibrord met in Jutland during the first Christian mission to Scandinavia around 725. Angantyr is described as the King of the Danes but it is unclear if this means all of them or just those in Jutland. The latter is more likely because we know that some parts of Denmark, such as the island of Bornholm, were still independent kingdoms as late as 900. Another kingdom was centred in Uppland, north of Lake Mälaren in Sweden, around the major pagan cult centre at Gamla Uppsala. Three vast burial mounds here are traditionally associated with the sixth-century Svear kings Aun, Egil and Adils of the semi-legendary Yngling dynasty. Two of the mounds which have been excavated have been dated to the fifth and sixth centuries AD and each contained the cremated remains of a high-ranking male. Slightly later cemeteries at nearby Vendel and Välsgarde, containing burials with exceptionally rich furnishings including fine armour and ships, probably also belonged to the Svear royal dynasty. Elaborately furnished burial mounds at Borre and Oseberg in Vestfold (west of Oslo Fjord) also suggest the establishment of a powerful royal dynasty in southern Norway in the century before the beginning of the Viking age. In the course of the Viking era these primitive and still precarious states would be forged into the medieval kingdoms of Denmark, Norway and Sweden.

TWO

Raids

The earliest recorded Viking raid was the attack on Portland, Wessex in about 789 in which the unfortunate reeve Beaduheard was killed. By 792 Viking raids were enough of a problem to cause the Mercian king Offa to organize coastal defences in Kent. Then in 793 came one of the most famous of all Viking raids, the attack on the wealthy Northumbrian monastery of St Cuthbert on the island of Lindisfarne. Some of the monks were killed and others taken captive, the altars of the church were despoiled but no serious structural damage was done and the monks appear to have had enough warning of the attack to hide the monastery's greatest treasures, including the magnificently illuminated *Lindisfarne Gospels* and the relics of St Cuthbert. The Frankish king Charlemagne tried to ransom the captured monks but we do not know if he succeeded. The next year the Vikings returned to attack the nearby monastery at Jarrow but a storm wrecked their fleet and those survivors who made it ashore were killed by the locals. In 795 Vikings ravaged the Scottish Hebridean islands, sacking the monastery on Iona, before moving on to raid the coast of Ireland. Four years later it was the turn of Charlemagne's mighty Frankish empire to suffer its first Viking raids when a fleet appeared off the coast of Aquitaine. In 800 a Frankish annalist complained that 'the sea was infested with pirates' and a few years later a papal legate on a mission to Northumbria was captured at sea and held to ransom.

To Christian western Europeans these attacks were a bolt from the blue. Under strong and capable rulers like Charlemagne and Offa, western Europe was experiencing a degree of peace, stability and modest prosperity such as it had not enjoyed since the days of the Roman Empire. No threat was perceived from the sea and everywhere ports, towns and monasteries were completely undefended. The sudden outbreak of Viking pirate raids was therefore deeply shocking, all the more so since the Vikings, being pagans, cared nothing for the spiritual sanctions which protected the property and personnel of the Church when Christian states were at war. Monasteries, the most important religious and cultural centres of early medieval Europe, suffered particularly severely from Viking attacks. Some European rulers, such as Charlemagne, reacted vigorously to the threat of Viking raids but these proved very difficult to combat effectively. Rivers could be blocked by fleets or fortified bridges but the open coastline remained desperately exposed. It was impossible to defend everywhere all of the time so, like the modern terrorist, the Vikings usually held the initiative, being able to choose the time and place of their attacks. For example, a Viking fleet which attacked Francia in 822 was twice driven off by coastguards but it eventually found a gap in the defences and sacked a village in Aquitaine. The Vikings' greatest advantage was their mobility. Their fine longships were fast under sail or oars and even fully loaded drew only a few inches of water, making them ideal for sudden beach landings or penetrating far inland along rivers. All too often, by the time the defenders had gathered in enough strength to counter-attack, the Vikings had taken their plunder and gone. Such was the fate of Charlemagne's counter-attack against the Danish king Godfred's attack on Frisia in 810: when his fleet and army arrived in the area Godfred was already back at home.

For forty years after the attacks on Portland and Lindisfarne, Viking raids continued to be small-scale affairs: hit-and-run attacks on monasteries and other targets on the open coast by fleets of up to about a dozen ships. This kind of raiding was a seasonal occupation which had to be fitted in to the pattern of the farming year – raids took place in the late spring between sowing and haymaking and in the autumn between the grain harvest and the onset of winter gales in December. Viking raiding entered a new and more serious phase in the 830s. Viking fleets became larger – thirty to thirty-five ships are recorded in the 830s, rising to over one hundred by the 850s – and much bolder as they began for the first time to probe their way inland along navigable rivers. In the 840s the Vikings also began to establish fortified winter camps, first in Ireland and Francia, then in England, from which they could make an early start to raiding in the spring and extend their activity later into the autumn.

Initially it was the Frankish empire which bore the brunt of the intensified raiding. The Vikings were always sensitive to political problems and quick to take advantage of them. When civil war broke out in 830 between the emperor Louis the Pious (r. 814–40) and his sons, the effectiveness of the coastal defences was fatally undermined. In 834 a Viking fleet sailed over 100 kilometres up the Rhine to sack the main Frankish port of Dorestad: they returned in each of the next three years. After sacking Nantes in 842, the Vikings established a permanent base on the island of Noirmoutier, near the mouth of the Loire, and thereafter were a permanent presence on Frankish territory for the next seventy years. The main areas of Viking activity in the Frankish empire were the valleys of the Seine and Loire and Flanders, Frisia and the Rhineland, all areas where navigable rivers offered raiders easy routes inland. Preoccupied as they were by dynastic conflicts, the empire's Carolingian rulers were rarely free to concentrate on dealing with the Viking threat and were frequently reduced to buying them off with tribute. Although this got rid of the Vikings in the short term, in the longer term it simply encouraged more attacks. Towns were left exposed to attack because kings such as Charles the Bald (r. 843–77) refused to allow them to build defences in case they should be turned into strongholds by rebel princes and vassals. For some of these rebels, such as Pippin II of Aquitaine (d. 864), the Vikings were even welcome as allies: he was later accused by the Franks of having adopted paganism and other Scandinavian customs. The Frankish defence was also hampered by what was a fundamental weakness of all early medieval military systems (including that of the Vikings). It was always relatively easy to raise an army to invade someone else's territory because this offered the prospect of plunder and payments of tribute to offset the risks and costs of warfare. Raising an army for a defensive campaign was quite another matter; even the great Charlemagne had problems in this regard. No plunder could be expected, yet the risks and costs were just as great, and while a soldier was away defending one part of the kingdom, his own home and lands were left unprotected and exposed to attack.

The Viking raids reached their peak in the period 878–92 when the Rhineland, the Ardennes, Flanders and the Seine valley were systematically ravaged. But the Franks were finally getting the measure of the Vikings. Able warrior kings such as Odo of the West Franks (France) and Arnulf of the East Franks (Germany) actively sought to bring the Vikings to battle and built fortresses and town walls across the whole of the region between the Seine and the Rhine. Faced with resistance wherever they went, and a severe famine in the winter of 891/2, the main Viking army in Francia withdrew to England in 892, where it fared no better. The worst of the Viking age was now over for the Franks, but armies of Viking diehards remained on the Seine and the Loire.

The base on the Loire brought the Iberian peninsula within range of Viking raids but this was not to be one of their happy hunting grounds. In 844 a Viking fleet attacked the wealthy and powerful Muslim emirate of Cordoba, sacking Lisbon and Cadiz before sailing up the River Guadalquivir and capturing Seville. The Vikings held Seville for six weeks before they were trapped and defeated by the Muslims with heavy loss of life. A second expedition from 859 to 862 under two famous Vikings, Hastein and Bjorn Ironside, penetrated the Mediterranean but, though it became the stuff of legends, it fared little better and lost two-thirds of its ships. Some Moors captured on this expedition finished up as slaves in Ireland. The Christian kingdoms of the north also offered stiff resistance and were generally left alone by the Vikings.

Raids on Ireland also intensified in the 830s. Larger Viking fleets began to arrive and for the first time sailed up Ireland's many navigable rivers, such as the Shannon, to attack areas far inland, causing widespread destruction. Few Irish monasteries escaped the Vikings' attentions and Armagh, the island's leading ecclesiastical centre, was sacked three times in 832 alone. Ireland in the early ninth century was divided into five competitive high kingdoms and dozens of unruly subkingdoms so there was no coordinated Irish response to the raids. By 841 the Vikings had become a permanent presence in Ireland, building fortified bases or *longphorts*, the most successful of which was Dublin. Once the Vikings settled down they became more vulnerable to counter-attack and Irish resistance became more effective: the capture and execution by the Irish of their warlord Turgeis in 845 and four major defeats in 847 led many Vikings to seek easier pickings on the Continent. In 853 Olaf, the son of a Norwegian king, made himself King of Dublin and under him the Vikings were gradually drawn into Irish political life, as local rulers such as Cerball, King of Ossory, sought them as allies in their interminable internecine struggles. After the death

23

of Olaf's successor, Ivar, in 873 Ireland experienced a long respite from raiding known as the Forty Years Rest while the Vikings concentrated their activities in England and the Frankish empire. It seemed as if the Irish had finally seen the last of the Vikings when they captured Dublin in 902 and watched them scramble for their ships. Many of the Scandinavian refugees from Ireland crossed the Irish Sea to settle quietly in north-west England.

Though it too faced larger Viking fleets from the 830s onwards, England suffered less severely from Viking raids than Ireland or the Frankish empire until 865 when a 'great heathen army' from Denmark invaded the kingdom of East Anglia. This differed from earlier Viking armies in that its aim was not simply to plunder but to conquer lands for settlement. The Danes forced the East Anglians to supply them with horses and the next year rode north to invade Northumbria, where two rivals for the throne had chosen this inopportune moment to begin a civil war. The Danes captured York, the Northumbrian capital, unopposed and when the two rival kings united to try to recapture the city in 867 they were defeated and killed. York became the capital of a Danish kingdom comprising all of

Northumbria between the Humber and the Tees. In 869 the Danes returned to East Anglia, defeating and capturing its King, Edmund. When the King refused to renounce Christianity or rule as a Danish puppet he was tortured to death, for which he was soon recognized as a martyr. The Anglo-Saxon kingdoms did not cooperate effectively against the invaders: the only attempt, a joint Mercian-West Saxon siege of the Danes in Nottingham in 868, was a failure. Wessex's turn came in 870, but after fighting five indecisive battles in quick succession the Danes withdrew, first to London then to York. Mercia proved a softer target when the Danes invaded in 872. Within two years the Mercian king, Burgred, had abdicated and the Danes appointed a puppet ruler as a caretaker until they should decide what to do with their conquest. It now seemed possible that the Danes would conquer the whole of England. In 874 the Danish army divided into two, one half, under Halfdan, returning to York and from there invading Bernicia (the unconquered part of Northumbria north of the Tees) and Scotland. In 877 Halfdan invaded Ireland, where he was killed: his followers were now more interested in settling the lands he had won around York than fighting, so the Northumbrians of Bernicia kept their independence. The other half of the Danish army, under Guthrum and others, moved to Cambridge and from there invaded Wessex in 875. By the winter of 878 the King of Wessex, Alfred the Great (r. 871–99), had been forced into hiding in the marshes of Somerset, but he rallied resistance to the Danes and later that year won a decisive victory at Edington, Wiltshire. The Danish King, Guthrum, agreed peace terms with Alfred, accepted baptism and withdrew to settle in East Anglia. Alfred used the peace to reform his army, build a fleet to challenge the Vikings at sea and stud his kingdom with fortified settlements called *burhs*. When a large Viking army invaded Wessex from the Low Countries in 892 it faced opposition and harassment at every turn and after four fruitless years it broke up, some of its members going to settle on the rich farmlands they had conquered in Mercia, Northumbria and East Anglia, others returning to the Continent.

The Viking raids in Scotland are less well documented than in Ireland, England and Francia but they followed a similar pattern. What is now modern Scotland was then divided between four ethnic groups – the Scots in Argyll, the Picts of the

Grampian Highlands, the Britons (i.e. Welsh) of Strathclyde and the Anglo-Saxons of Northumbria south-east of the Forth. As far as can be told, there were two main areas of activity: the Northern and Western Isles, where monasteries such as Iona faced repeated attacks, and the central lowlands. Probably by the middle of the ninth century Norwegians had begun to settle in the islands but they were never able to establish a foothold in the central valley, where the Scots were also expanding against the Picts. The evidence does not exist to say why this was.

There is no evidence that Wales suffered any serious Viking raids until about 855 when Anglesey was ravaged by Irish-based Vikings. Stiff Welsh resistance led by Rhodri Mawr (r. 844–77), king of the leading Welsh kingdom of Gwynedd, prevented any attempts by the Vikings at colonization. Raids from Ireland tailed off in the 870s, reflecting the decline of Viking power there but Wales was often affected by the 'overspill' of raids which were directed primarily at England. The worst period of Viking raids for Wales came much later, in the late tenth and early eleventh centuries.

THREE

The Wrath of God?

Naturally enough, contemporary writers tried to explain the terrifying outbreak of Viking raiding. While still stunned by the appalling news of the Viking attack on Lindisfarne in 793, the Anglo-Saxon scholar Alcuin wrote 'never before has such terror been seen in Britain as we have suffered by this pagan people'. It was not so much the bloodshed and destruction that alarmed Alcuin, though that was serious enough, but the fact that St Cuthbert had not intervened from above to protect his monastery. The attack could only be interpreted as God's punishment for some terrible sin. What was worse, Alcuin concluded, if somewhere as holy as Lindisfarne could not expect the protection of the saints, then nowhere was safe. This interpretation of Viking raids as an expression of the wrath of God was generally accepted by early medieval Europeans and was frequently reiterated by later writers at times of particularly serious attacks. A stout defence was only part of the solution to Viking attacks: what was needed above all was to win back God's favour by a return to true Christian values. For example, Alfred the Great's well-known attempts to revive learning and improve the quality of the English clergy have to be understood in this context.

The causes of the Viking raids have seemed much less obvious to modern historians. Until recently, the Viking expansion was most commonly explained in terms of land-hunger caused by Scandinavia's growing population. In the centuries immediately preceding the Viking age new settlements were being created, more land was being brought under cultivation and iron production was increasing steadily to meet the demand for tools and weapons. Considering Scandinavia's lack of good arable land it might be expected that the pressure of this increasing population would soon make itself felt. Both Norway and Sweden have seen considerable emigration, mainly to the USA, in periods of population growth in recent times and there is also plentiful evidence of migrations out of Scandinavia before the Viking era. The Cimbri and Teutones who invaded the Roman Empire in 113 BC originated in

Jutland as did the Angles and Jutes who settled in Britain in the fifth century AD. Several of the Germanic peoples who invaded the Roman Empire at this time, including the Burgundians, Goths and Vandals, also had historical traditions that they too had once lived in Scandinavia. The sixth-century Gothic historian Jordanes recognized this pattern of frequent migrations out of Scandinavia, which he described as the 'womb of peoples'.

But, while it is true that the Viking age did see substantial emigration out of Scandinavia, the first phase of Viking activity was dominated by pirates not settlers. More than half a century had passed from the time of the first attacks in the 790s before any major Scandinavian settlements were made in the Scottish islands. Vikings had certainly visited the Faroe Islands before 825 but there is no conclusive evidence of settlement that early and Iceland was only settled in the 870s, around the same time that the Danish settlement of eastern England began. Norwegian settlement of north-west England dates to the first decades of the tenth century, as does the Danish settlement in Normandy. In Ireland there was never any extensive Scandinavian settlement outside of a few coastal enclaves such as Dublin,

Wexford and Limerick. The Scandinavian Rus (of Swedish origin), who won control of a vast area of eastern Europe, remained a minority warrior-elite lording it over a subject Slavic population. Land-hunger, therefore, cannot have been a decisive factor in the outbreak of Viking raiding. It is more likely that it was the success of these raids which opened the way for Scandinavian settlement overseas.

The success of Viking raiding was in no small part due to the mobility which their splendid ships gave them. (Divisions among their enemies was the other major factor.) This has led some historians to seek a technological explanation for the Viking expansion. According to this line of argument, the eighth century saw the Scandinavians perfect the technology of the seagoing sailing ship. Before this time they had relied on large rowing ships which, while adequate for piracy and transport in sheltered coastal waters, were not suited to long-distance raiding. The adoption of the sail, therefore, opened up enormous new opportunities for raiding, of which the Scandinavians were not slow to avail themselves. It goes almost without saying that seaworthy ships were a prerequisite for Viking raiding, but this does not mean that they actually were a cause of it. The Scandinavians do appear to be have been just about the last Europeans to adopt sailing ships and it is also true that the earliest-known Scandinavian sailing ship, the Oseberg ship, was not built until about 820. However, late seventh-century stone carvings from Gotland do show sailing ships, as does a small carving of around the same date from Jutland. It is possible, therefore, that the Scandinavians had possessed suitable ships for over a century before the start of Viking raiding. Also, sea forays out of Scandinavia were not unknown before the Viking age, the earliest recorded one being an attack by the Heruls (from Jutland) on the lower Rhine in 287. In the fifth century the Heruls raided as far south as Spain, and in the sixth century attacks by the Danes or Götar are recorded on Frisia and the lower Rhine.

A more significant factor in the outbreak of Viking raiding was trade: it is certainly the most satisfactory explanation of Swedish expansion east of the Baltic Sea. The relative political stability of eighth-century Europe led to a modest economic recovery and an increase in trade with Scandinavia, which was an important source of luxury goods such as furs, walrus ivory, amber and probably other goods such as hides. By the mid-eighth century the Swedes had already established themselves at Finnish or Slav settlements such as Staraja Ladoga in north-east Russia. These were probably used as bases for the collection of furs, either purchased or extorted as tribute from the native peoples, which the Swedes then used to supply the western European market. At about the same time, Arab merchants were also penetrating Russia from the south along the River Volga. The merchants introduced high quality silver coins, called *dirhems*, into circulation in eastern Europe, giving the Swedes an incentive to push further east to establish direct contact with this new and lucrative market.

As the existence of piracy necessarily implies the existence of something worth plundering, the increase in trade between Scandinavia and western Europe may also have encouraged Viking raids. Even the earliest Viking raiders seem to have known which places to attack, suggesting that they had already become familiar with western Europe's unguarded coastal monasteries and ports in the course of peaceful trading expeditions. The Scandinavians were certainly known to the Anglo-

Saxons and Franks before they started raiding. Poor Beaduheard thought the Norwegians at Portland were merchants and according to Alcuin, writing in 793, the Northumbrians were already so familiar with the Scandinavians that their hairstyles had become the height of fashion.

The main cause of the outbreak of Viking raiding was, however, political developments in Scandinavia itself. Power in Scandinavian society had for centuries been becoming more and more concentrated in fewer and fewer hands as chiefdoms became amalgamated into kingdoms. At the beginning of the Viking age these kingdoms were still highly unstable. While the opportunities to become an independent ruler were decreasing, Scandinavian society possessed an unusually large class of men who could aspire to kingship. In theory, kings were elective and anyone who had inherited royal blood from either his father's or his mother's family was eligible to be considered: illegitimacy was no bar to succession either. As a result there could be many potential claimants for a throne and succession disputes were very common. Joint kings were a common solution where rival claimants enjoyed equal support and were prepared to compromise, but disputed successions often led to civil war. If they were lucky enough to survive, the losers in these conflicts would be forced into exile but, being possessed of the charisma of royal blood, all was not lost to them. One possible course of action was that taken by Harald Klak, a Danish king chased into exile in 813. In 814 he sought the support of the Frankish emperor Louis the Pious for a bid to regain his throne. Louis, mindful that if the Danes were fighting among themselves they would have less time to raid his empire, was happy to oblige. Others, though, used the prestige that came from their possession of royal blood to attract a warrior band and go plundering. With luck, an exile could win a small fortune, a reputation as a great warrior and a loyal armed following with which to make a new bid for power at home. One of the most successful Vikings in this respect was Olaf Tryggvason who after five years of successful raiding in England returned home to Norway and seized power in 995. Other exiles, such as Erik Bloodaxe, may have decided that if they could not rule at home, they would seek a kingdom overseas. Erik, driven off the Norwegian throne by his brother Håkon the Good in about 936, spent several years raiding in Scotland before establishing himself as King of York in 948. Ivar, Halfdan and the other leaders of the Danish 'Great Army' which invaded England in 865 seem to have intended to found overseas kingdoms from the outset of their careers. Scandinavian kings were rulers of men rather than territory and it is significant that the leaders of the 'Great Army' were recognized as kings by their followers even though they had no kingdoms. Returning exiles were a destabilizing influence in the Viking kingdoms and a constant problem for established rulers who also led plundering raids of their own in order to strengthen their own positions and reputations. The centralization of power also affected the Scandinavian chieftain class, which found its traditional autonomy increasingly undermined. For chieftains, raiding offered a way to maintain their status and opportunities for independent action. Emigration offered them the chance to retain their autonomy on lands they had won by right of conquest or, in the case of Iceland and Greenland, which were previously uninhabited. The outbreak of Viking raiding is therefore best interpreted as a consequence of the competitive and predatory society which had developed in Scandinavia in the late Iron Age.

FOUR

Rape and Pillage?

The traditional view of the Vikings was that they were bloodthirsty pirates pouring in their tens of thousands out of Scandinavia intent on destruction, rape, pillage and slaughter. In the last forty years there has been a tendency to downplay the violent side of their activity. The Vikings, it is argued, were the victims of a bad press: their destructiveness was greatly exaggerated by hostile monastic chroniclers who were biased against them because they were pagans and because of their predilection for looting monasteries; the Vikings were no more violent than anyone else in early medieval Europe and should be regarded primarily as traders, settlers and craftsmen rather than pirates. Which view of the Vikings is the correct one?

The fact is that there is a great deal of truth in both views. The term 'Viking' has come in modern times to be applied to all early medieval Scandinavians and it is directly as a result of this that the controversy has arisen. As used originally in the Viking age itself, the word was applied only to someone who went *i víking*, that is someone whose occupation was piracy. The earliest use of the word predates the Viking age by some years and it was not even used exclusively to describe Scandinavian pirates. Most Viking age Scandinavians were not Vikings at all in this original sense of the word but were simply peaceful farmers, craftsmen and merchants. However, those Scandinavians who chose piracy and war as their profession (i.e. who became *vikingr*), and joined the raids on western Europe, must have been prepared to use whatever degree of violence was necessary to achieve their ends: *viking* was by definition a violent activity. It should be said in passing that the Viking raids were in no way a campaign of Scandinavians against the rest of Europe. Scandinavians were themselves often the victims of Viking raids and on occasions English, Irish, Franks, Bretons and Slavs all participated in raids as allies of the Vikings, often against their own countryfolk.

To what extent, if at all, were Viking warriors more violent than their European contemporaries? It is certain that Christian Europeans of the day could wage war with great ruthlessness, as Charlemagne's execution of 4,500 pagan Saxon rebels at Verden in 782 clearly shows; moreover, plundering and tribute gathering were carried out by Christian armies as well as by the Vikings. But western Europe was more peaceful at the end of the eighth century than it had been at any time since the fall of the western Roman Empire over 400 years previously. One sign of this general sense of security is that, away from disputed borderlands, fortifications of any sort were rare. The outbreak of Viking raids changed this dramatically, making the threat of violence an everyday concern for the inhabitants of large areas of Europe for years on end. One of the least orderly parts of western Europe, early medieval Ireland, was divided into a multitude of rival kingdoms which were frequently at war, yet in the period 831–919 Irish annals record only 16 instances of natives plundering and burning as against 110 by the Vikings. In times of war between Christians the property and personnel of the Church were protected by powerful spiritual sanctions. Even in Ireland, where the monks of rival monasteries sometimes took up arms to settle their differences, churches were rarely plundered. As pagans, however, the Vikings felt no such restraints, though they targeted churches and monasteries because of their wealth rather than from any active hostility to Christianity itself. Incidents such as the slaughter of 68 monks at the Scottish monastery of Iona in 806 led to the abandonment of hundreds of monasteries during the ninth century. Contemporary chroniclers recorded many incidents of wanton destruction and killing on a scale previously unheard of by the writers. Recounting Viking raids in the Rhineland in 884 the chronicler of the abbey of St Vaast spoke of towns in flames and roads littered with the bodies of men, women, children and babies. People suspected of knowing the whereabouts of hidden valuables could expect to be tortured, to death if they did not crack. Such was the fate of Blathmacc, the prior of Iona, in 825. Especially in Ireland, thousands of people were systematically rounded up and herded to the slave markets. Thus even the Vikings' 'peaceful' trading activities were supplied with their most valuable commodities by violence. Despite their understandable hostility towards the Vikings, there is little reason to believe that these accounts, most of them written by monks, greatly exaggerate the horrors of a major Viking raid. Accounts of Viking forays written in the more sophisticated cultural atmospheres of the Byzantine empire and the Islamic world also record acts of horrific violence and destruction. It is perhaps significant in this respect that the Vikings are scarcely ever accused of rape, which we might expect to be added to the charges against them if contemporary writers had simply been out to blacken their name in all possible ways. Not all Viking raids were highly destructive, however. With the common practice of *strandhögg*, a small-scale beach landing to seize untended cattle and other provisions, the perpetrators would hope to land and escape undetected, so avoiding a fight. Viking armies were by no means eager for battle (you could be injured or killed and you might lose) and were generally happy to be bought off with payments of tribute. Yet the Vikings' ability to extract these payments depended ultimately on their proven willingness to use extreme violence.

Christian Europeans' perception of Viking raiders as extremely fierce is echoed in the Vikings' own skaldic poetry. As the court poets of Viking Scandinavia, the skalds' function was to compose panegyric poems glorifying the military achievements of their royal or aristocratic patrons. The modern reader might find skaldic verse gratuitously violent, dwelling as it does on ravens and wolves feasting on corpses and the weeping of widows and orphans, but it is certain that it was very much to the taste of the Scandinavian warrior elite. It is from skaldic verse that we know of the 'blood eagle', the Viking custom of hacking open a captive's rib-cage on either side of the spine so that his lungs could be torn out to form a pair of bloody wings. It is thought that the practice was a sacrifice to the pagan war god, Odin. Some historians regard the blood eagle as a literary invention but the evidence of the Vikings' use of torture suggests they were certainly capable of it. And it has been rightly pointed out that the blood eagle is no more horrific than the old English punishment for traitors of hanging, drawing and quartering. For this reason we should be very wary of concluding that the Vikings were uniquely inhuman. The Vikings were tough people from a barbarian society in which violence was recognized as the surest way to wealth and power; there should be no surprise that they glorified it and were quick to have resort to it.

The Viking armies which ravaged western Europe in the ninth century had a loose and flexible organization. The basic unit of a Viking army was the *lið]*, the private warrior retinue of a chieftain or king, the size of which varied according to the wealth and status of its leader. The warriors of a *lið* formed a *félag* (fellowship) bonded by oaths of mutual loyalty and agreement to share the spoils of war. Discipline was probably maintained by the individual warrior's fear of dishonour if he abandoned his comrades in the thick of battle. A *lið* could operate independently as a raiding band and the great Viking armies were simply a group of *liðr* which had joined together for a common purpose. Once the campaign was concluded the army broke up into its respective *liðr*, which might take their loot and go home, settle on conquered lands or move on to join another Viking army somewhere else. Some warriors would be accompanied on campaign by their wives. Though women did not fight, they performed a useful function, cooking and tending the sick and wounded. The great Danish armies which conquered England under Svein Forkbeard and Cnut in the early eleventh century were more centrally organized and included a high proportion of mercenaries.

The size of the Viking armies has proved very difficult to estimate because most contemporary witnesses found it easier to count ships than warriors. Thus the Anglo-Saxon chronicler described the Danish force which arrived in Kent in 892 as being 250 ships strong. Estimates of the numbers of warriors in Viking armies are rare in continental sources and quite unknown in Anglo-Saxon ones. There is also the problem of establishing the reliability of these sources. Some modern historians have argued that early medieval chroniclers habitually exaggerated the size of the Viking fleets and that in reality their armies were small, numbering in the hundreds rather than thousands. While it is impossible not to suspect some contemporary writers of exaggeration – for example, the French monk Abbo who gives the size of a Viking army besieging Paris from 885 to 886 as numbering 40,000 men and 700 ships – there is little hard evidence that this was a universal fault. For the most part there is remarkable consistency between accounts written independently in different parts of Europe as to the size of Viking fleets, strongly suggesting that the figures we are given, while no doubt approximate in most cases, are broadly accurate. Irish, Anglo-Saxon and Frankish sources all agree that Viking fleets were small (up to about

35 ships) before the mid-830s, that from then until about 850 they numbered in the region of 50 to 100 ships and that from then until Viking activity tailed off in the 890s, fleets of 200 to 350 ships were common, though many smaller fleets were still recorded too.

Typical Viking warships appear to have carried crews of between twenty-five and sixty. The best preserved of all Viking longships is the Gokstad ship, built in Norway around 895 to 900. The 23.5 metre-long ship had a single square sail and sixteen pairs of oars, suggesting a minimum crew of thirty-two plus the steersman. However, a rack along the gunwale carried two shields between each oar port, indicating that the ship actually carried a double crew of sixty-four, to allow rowing in shifts. The slightly later longship from Ladby in Denmark also had sixteen pairs of oars but was much narrower than the Gokstad ship so probably could not carry many supernumeraries, while an early eleventh-century longship from Skuldelev (known as 'wreck 5') had only twelve or thirteen pairs of oars. Late in the Viking age a type of super-longship with thirty pairs of oars or more, known as a *drakkar*, came into use. The most famous of these, King Olaf Tryggvason's

Long Serpent, had thirty-four pairs of oars and could carry a crew of several hundred. Wrecks of such ships have been discovered at Skuldelev and Roskilde in Denmark.

If we err on the side of caution and assume that the smaller Danish longships were more typical than the Gokstad ship, then the fleet which invaded Kent in 892 probably carried upwards of 5,000 men, a substantial force by early medieval standards but not improbably large when it is considered that in about 900 the Anglo-Saxon kingdom of Wessex alone could raise just over 27,000 armed men for garrison duty and maintain a standing field army and a fleet as well. Early medieval armies had to live off the land and the evidence indicates that large Viking armies split up into smaller units to forage and plunder whenever they were based in one place for any length of time. The Danish fleets which operated against England in the late tenth and early eleventh centuries were smaller than those of the ninth century – Cnut conquered England between 1015 and 1016 with a fleet of only 160 ships – but they would have included many of the new *drakkars*, so the size of the armies was probably very similar. These figures are comparable to the strength, estimated at around 6,000, of the Norman army which conquered England in 1066.

Though their armies may have been relatively large by the standards of the day, there were certainly not vast hordes of Vikings pouring out of Scandinavia. Vikings tended to concentrate in particular places at particular times. While the Danish 'Great Army' was active in England from 865 to 878, Francia enjoyed a respite from large-scale Viking raids. When Viking activity was at its most intensive in Francia between 879 and 892, it was England's turn for a respite. It was very rare for more than one or two large Viking armies to be active at the same time, so it seems unlikely that there could ever have been more than about 10,000 Vikings active in the whole of western Europe even at the peak of their raids between 850 and 900, and most of the time there would have been considerably fewer.

FIVE

Settlement and Assimilation

At the beginning of the tenth century it must have seemed to most Christian western Europeans that the Vikings would soon be a thing of the past: Ireland had been cleared of Vikings, in England they were too busy tilling the land to make much trouble and only small Viking armies remained on the Seine and Loire in Francia. But the lull in activity was only temporary.

The threat of the Seine Vikings was ended permanently in 911 when King Charles the Simple (r. 898–922) made their leader Rollo (d. *c.* 925) count of Rouen in return for his agreement to defend the area against other Viking bands. Normandy, as Rollo's territories came to be known (from Nordmannia or 'Northman's Land'), created problems of its own but at least they were the familiar ones of dynastic and territorial ambition which all medieval kings faced from over-mighty subjects. But not all the Vikings in Francia were ready to settle down. Some of Rollo's followers left to join the more aggressive Loire Vikings in raiding Brittany, which had escaped relatively lightly during the ninth century. Their attacks became so ferocious that in 919 the Breton nobles simply threw in the towel and fled to England and Francia. Within a year the Vikings, under their leader Rognvald, had conquered all of Brittany. But Brittany was not destined to become a second Normandy. Rognvald and his followers were not remotely interested in creating an orderly principality and they continued to live by plunder. Helped by the English king Athelstan, duke Alan Barbetorte returned to Brittany in 936 and in 939 finally succeeded in driving the Vikings out. Small-scale Viking raids continued into the early eleventh century but as far as continental Europe is concerned Alan's victory effectively marked the end of the Viking age. The Scandinavian settlers – most of them Danes – in Normandy were a minority among the native Franks and they quickly began to adopt Frankish culture and language, including conversion to Christianity.

49

Monasteries which had been abandoned because of Viking raids in the ninth century were reoccupied and rebuilt, often with the help of Norman rulers. Immigration from Scandinavia ended in the 960s and trade links between Normandy and Scandinavia had been abandoned by 1000. The last evidence of Scandinavian influence in Normandy is the presence of a Norwegian poet at the ducal court in 1025. Long before 1066, Normandy had become a completely French principality.

Having left Ireland in undignified haste in 902, the Vikings returned in force in 914 and were soon re-established at Dublin and other ports such as Waterford, Wexford, Limerick and Cork. Yet, though their raids resumed with a vengeance, they made no lasting conquests or settlements beyond these coastal enclaves. The kings of Dublin were often diverted by their ambitions to rule York and by wars with the other Viking towns while Irish resistance was increasingly well organized. From the 940s onward, the Vikings found their activities increasingly curtailed and one by one their towns came under the domination of Irish kings. In 968 King Mathgamain of Dal Cais temporarily expelled the Vikings from Limerick. However, this was an unusual reaction: generally, Irish kings recognized the value of the Norse towns for the trade they brought to Ireland and the tribute they were prepared to pay in order to maintain their independence. Being possessed of strong fleets and a martial spirit, the Vikings were also valued by Irish kings as allies in their internecine struggles for the High Kingship.

In 997 Dublin, the richest and largest of the Norse towns, came under the overlordship of Brian Boru, the powerful King of Munster. In 1002 Brian became High King and set about trying to impose his authority throughout Ireland. To try to preserve its independence, Dublin's king, Silttric Silkbeard, built an alliance of Leinster and the Norse earldom of Orkney. The alliance was defeated by Brian at the battle of Clontarf in 1014 but he was himself killed. Clontarf is still popularly regarded as marking the end of the Viking age in Ireland but in reality the battle has little historical significance. Brian's death changed nothing for the Norse towns: they remained, as they had been for decades, dominated by the Irish. The Norse settlers were by this time losing their Scandinavian character through conversion to Christianity, intermarriage with the

Irish and adoption of the Gaelic language. The Irish now knew the inhabitants of the Norse towns as 'Ostmen' ('men of the east' [of Ireland]) to distinguish them from native Scandinavians. The Ostmen preserved their distinctive Irish-Norse character into the mid-thirteenth century, by which time they had become assimilated either to the native Irish population or the English settlers who had followed in the wake of the Anglo-Norman conquest of 1169 to 1171.

When Alfred the Great died in 899, England was almost evenly divided between the Anglo-Saxons and the Danes. All of eastern England from the Thames estuary north to the River Tees was under Danish rule. Characteristic placename elements, such as *-by* and *-thorpe*, show that Danish settlement was particularly dense in East Anglia, Yorkshire and in the area of the Five Boroughs of Lincoln, Stamford, Leicester, Nottingham and Derby, but nowhere did they form the majority of the population. The Danes introduced their own legal customs into the area under their control, from which it became known as the 'Danelaw'. The Danelaw divided into many small kingdoms and chiefdoms, the largest of which were East Anglia and the kingdom of York. Shortly after

900, Norwegians, many of whom had been driven out of Ireland, began to settle in northwest England. Little is known about this movement but the northwest was a sparsely populated area at the time and on the whole the settlement appears to have been accomplished peacefully. Alfred the Great had taken upon himself the leadership of all the Anglo-Saxons who were not living under Danish rule (and he negotiated favourable treatment for those who were). Alfred forged a strong alliance with the Mercians by marrying his daughter Æthelflæd to their ruler, Æthelred, and also cultivated close relations with the independent Northumbrians in Bernicia. Alfred's son and successor, Edward the Elder (r. 899–924), built on his achievements and in 912 he began a methodical conquest of the Danelaw. He was ably supported throughout by his sister Æthelflæd who led the Mercians personally to capture Derby in 917. Edward was not seen as a liberator by all the Anglo-Saxons in the Danelaw; many fought with the Danes against him. Now that the Danes had homes and property to defend, they had lost their main military advantage over the Anglo-Saxons: their mobility. Politically disunited, the Danes failed to mount a coordinated defence and the superior resources and organization of Wessex soon told. By the autumn of 918 Edward had conquered all of the Danelaw south of the Humber estuary. On Æthelflæd's death the following year, Edward formally annexed Mercia to Wessex. Those Anglo-Saxons who had fought with the Danes had been right – Edward was not leading an Anglo-Saxon *re*conquest of the Danelaw, he was leading a West Saxon takeover of England. That takeover was completed by Edward's son Athelstan (924–39).

The end of Viking power in England appeared to be in sight when the Danes of York offered to submit to Æthelflæd in 918 but she died before the offer could be acted upon and the following year York was seized by Ragnald, a Norwegian-Irish Viking from Dublin. A succession crisis in 927 gave Athelstan the opportunity to capture York and, when he annexed Bernicia in the same year, to become the first king to rule all of England. When Olaf Guthfrithsson of Dublin, in alliance with the Scots and Strathclyde Britons, tried to regain York in 937 he was crushingly defeated by Athelstan at the battle of Brunanburh, somewhere in the north of England. But Olaf did finally succeed in recapturing York when Athelstan died in 939 and in a daring campaign even added the Five Boroughs to his domains. But it was an ephemeral achievement and York was back in English hands by 944. York was returned to Viking rule for the last time in 948 when it was seized by Erik Bloodaxe, an exiled King of Norway with a fearsome reputation. Erik faced competition from Olaf Sihtricsson of Dublin and the English king Eadred and he was never able to rule securely. In 954 Erik was driven out of York and killed in an ambush as he fled.

Even before Erik's death, the Scandinavian settlers in England had begun to be assimilated to the native population through intermarriage and conversion to Christianity. Assimilation was aided in England by the similarities between the Old Norse and Old English languages. The Danes of the Five Boroughs had been dismayed to come under the rule of a pagan Norwegian in 940 and welcomed their return to English rule as liberation. Despite this, the Danelaw would retain a distinctive character for about 200 years after King Edgar had given the Danes legal autonomy in 970 to 974 as a reward for their loyalty to the crown.

But England's Viking age was far from over. A sudden shortage of silver in Scandinavia, caused by the exhaustion of the Islamic world's silver mines, and political instability in Norway and Denmark led to a resumption of Viking raiding on England in the 980s. At first these were on a small scale, conducted mainly by pirates from the Norwegian settlements in the Isle of Man and the Scottish islands. Then in the 990s came a series of well-organized, large-scale raids under royal leadership. England's king, Æthelred 'the Unready' (r. 978–1016), was an able administrator but he was a schemer and a poor soldier. As a result he could neither win the trust of his subjects nor provide them with inspiring and purposeful leadership in war. The English defences were soon run ragged and Æthelred was reduced to buying the Vikings off with huge payments of tribute, known later as 'Danegeld'. The Danish King, Svein Forkbeard (r. 986–1014) used this tribute to finance yet more raids. Finally, observing the collapse of English resistance, he decided upon the conquest of England in 1013. Only London put up much of a fight, but it too surrendered when Æthelred fled to Normandy at Christmas. England had in effect paid for its own conquest, but Svein's triumph was short-lived. A few weeks later he was dead, the English invited Æthelred back from exile and Svein's son and appointed successor, Cnut, was forced to flee. Cnut returned to claim his inheritance in 1015 but found the English defence reinvigorated by the leadership of Æthelred's spirited son, Edmund Ironside. The two fought one another across the length and breadth of southern England until Cnut finally won a decisive victory at the battle of Ashingdon, Essex, in October 1016. Edmund and Cnut agreed to divide the kingdom but, gravely wounded at Ashingdon, Edmund died within a few weeks and Cnut was accepted as king of all England (r. 1016–35). Under Cnut, England became part of a Scandinavian empire which included Denmark, Norway and Sweden. Cnut taxed the English heavily: normally this would be enough to ruin the reputation of any king of England but the English were grateful for his restoration of peace and orderly government and they remembered him as a just and pious ruler. Though Cnut's leading supporters were rewarded with English titles and lands, his conquest did not usher in another wave of Danish settlement. Most of Cnut's soldiers were mercenaries; their work successfully concluded, they took their pay and went home.

Cnut's successors were talentless nonentities. After his death his empire quickly fell apart, and in

England Æthelred's son Edward the Confessor restored the house of Wessex in 1042. Edward died childless in 1066, so bringing about the last Viking interventions in English history. The English chose Harold Godwinson for their king, but the throne was also claimed by Harald Hardrada, King of Norway, and William the Conqueror, Duke of Normandy. Harald moved first, landing in the Humber with 300 ships, defeating the English at Fulford Gate on 20 September and taking York. Harold marched north with incredible speed and surprised the Norwegians in camp at Stamford Bridge, near York, on 25 September. Harald was killed and his army was annihilated, so the *Anglo-Saxon Chronicle* tells us: only twenty-four ships were needed to take the survivors home. A few days later Harold marched back south to his own death in battle at Hastings against William. Might Harold have won at Hastings without the distraction of the Norwegian invasion? We might suspect so but the outcome of battle is always uncertain. Harald Hardrada's claim to the English throne was inherited by the Danish king, Svein Estrithson – who gave ineffectual support to rebellions against William in 1069 to 1070 and in 1075 – and then by his son Cnut II. In 1085 Cnut began to gather a huge fleet for an invasion of England but it never sailed. There was little enthusiasm in Denmark for the expedition and in 1086 Cnut was assassinated. The Viking threat to England was finally over. Linked to the Continent as never before by the Norman Conquest, England decisively drifted out of the Scandinavian orbit it had occupied for nearly 300 years.

The area in which the Viking age could be said to have continued longest was Scotland. Scandinavian settlement in Shetland, Orkney and Caithness in the ninth century had been so dense that all trace of the earlier Pictish inhabitants was lost: virtually all placenames in these areas have Scandinavian origins and a Norse dialect, Norn, was spoken in Orkney and Shetland until the eighteenth century. Around 870 Rognvald of Møre established an earldom in Orkney. Though Orkney was theoretically subject to the Norwegian kings it was the end of the eleventh century before they made their authority there a reality. The earls became powerful rulers in their own right. The second earl, Sigurd the Mighty (d. 892), began the expansion of the earldom, conquering Caithness and Sutherland. The earldom reached the height of its power under Sigurd the Stout (r. 985–1014), who brought the Norse settlements in the Hebrides under his control, and Thorfinn the Mighty (r. *c.* 1020–65), who conquered Ross in 1035. Thorfinn was also the first Orkney earl known to have ruled in the Shetland Islands, which previously had either been independent or been ruled from Norway.

Far to the south, in the Irish Sea, another Norse state developed on the Isle of Man. Under Godred Crovan (r. 1079–95) the kingdom of Man controlled the Hebrides and, briefly, Dublin. The kings of Norway had long claimed sovereignty over the Hebrides and Man but they had even less influence there than they had in Orkney, whose earls at least recognized Norwegian sovereignty even if they took little notice of it. The murder of one of his officials in the Hebrides in 1097 convinced King Magnus Barelegs (r. 1093–1103) that the time had come to enforce royal authority in the islands. In 1098 Magnus took a fleet to Orkney, deposed the earls and replaced them with his own son, Sigurd, then brutally ravaged the Hebrides and conquered the Isle of Man. But Magnus' achievement was short-lived. After his death on a Viking raid in Ireland, the kingdom of Man reasserted itself and Norwegian authority in the islands entered a gradual decline, creating a power vacuum in which old-fashioned Viking pirates, like Svein Asleifarson of Gairsay in Orkney, could continue to flourish long after they had been driven off the seas elsewhere. The last Norse pirate raid on the long-suffering monastery on Iona took place as late as 1210.

By the early twelfth century the Norse settlers in the Hebrides and Man were beginning to be assimilated into the native Gaelic-speaking populations: as in Ireland and England the main agent of assimilation was conversion to Christianity and intermarriage. One sign of this process was the rise to power of Somerled, a chieftain from Argyll of mixed Norse and Gaelic descent, who won control of the southern Hebrides from the kingdom of Man in 1156. The Scottish kings hoped to benefit from Somerled's ambitions but he preferred to recognize the sovereignty of the distant kings of Norway. But the Scots were not to be denied and their influence in the Hebrides steadily increased in the thirteenth century until in 1263 King Håkon IV led the 'Great Fleet' west to reassert Norwegian authority. After an indecisive skirmish with the Scots at Largs on the Clyde, Håkon, who was now ailing, withdrew to

Orkney where he died. His successor had more pressing problems and in 1266 he ceded the Hebrides and the Isle of Man to Scotland in return for 4,000 marks and an annuity. The last vestige of Norse power in Scotland was ended when Orkney and Shetland were ceded to Scotland by Denmark (which had ruled them since 1397) in 1469. Even today, however, Orkney and Shetland islanders retain a strong sense of their Scandinavian origins.

Despite the success of the Vikings in conquering and settling large parts of western Europe in the ninth and tenth centuries no part of it was permanently Scandinavianized as a result. The Scandinavians who settled there during the Viking age all, sooner or later, were assimilated by the native populations and lost their Scandinavian identity. What, then, was the impact of the Vikings on western Europe? At the general level, the Viking raids caused a great deal of short-term economic and cultural damage both in the British Isles and Francia. Hundreds of monasteries were abandoned and an untold quantity of works of art and manuscripts were lost, yet in the tenth century monasticism made a full and vigorous recovery. Many towns and villages were burned and looted but in an age when most building was in wood, much of this damage could be easily made good. The only two towns which are known to have been permanently abandoned during the Viking age, the Frankish ports of Quentovic and Dorestad, failed not because of Viking raids but because the rivers which gave access to them became unnavigable. Country people must have suffered considerable hardship through the loss of crops and livestock. The loss of manpower in battle or to slave raiders must also have been a severe economic blow to farming families. This human cost should not be underestimated, but the Viking age was by no means an unmitigated disaster for western Europe. In the wake of the raiders came merchants. The flow of plunder and tribute enriched Scandinavia and stimulated demand for European luxuries such as wine, glass, weapons and fine pottery. It was not only Scandinavian merchants who benefited: Anglo-Saxons and Frisians braved pirate attacks to trade at Scandinavian ports such as Hedeby in Denmark and Birka in Sweden. In Ireland, the Viking *longphorts* at Dublin and elsewhere developed into the island's first towns. The trade which the Vikings brought tied Ireland more closely into the European economy than it had ever been before. In England old established towns such as York benefited from new trade links and the country enjoyed a boom in trade with Scandinavia after its conquest by Cnut in 1016.

The political impact of the Viking raids was considerable. In Britain the Vikings disrupted the existing power structures, paving the way for the emergence of the unified kingdoms of England and Scotland. Although the Scots lost lands in the Hebrides to Scandinavian settlers, their neighbours, the Picts, Northumbrians and the Britons of Strathclyde, were weakened more, enabling the Scots to extend their control to most of northern Britain. By destroying the Anglo-Saxon kingdoms of East Anglia, Northumbria and Mercia, the Vikings made possible the unification of England by Wessex in the tenth century. The Danish settlements in eastern England also had a major influence on the development of the English language, which acquired hundreds of loan words from Old Norse, including bark, egg, skill, sky, sister, take and window. The Vikings' political impact on the Continent is harder to gauge. They are sometimes blamed for causing the break-up of the Carolingian empire but the dynamic for this was essentially dynastic. The Vikings certainly did benefit from the civil wars caused by the break-up of the empire and by so often demonstrating the impotence of the Carolingian dynasty they hastened its decline and fall. The Vikings also broke the power of Brittany, which had successfully maintained its independence against the Carolingians, leading ultimately to its absorption by France in the Middle Ages. The most long-lasting impact of the Vikings on the Continent, however, was in the foundation of the duchy of Normandy. In the late eleventh and early twelfth centuries, the Normans were to play a decisive role in the history of England, France, Italy and the Crusades.

SIX

West to Vinland

It was in the North Atlantic Ocean that the Vikings showed the full potential of their seafaring abilities. This was not the realm of the sleek longships; the ships they used for these voyages were stocky, sturdy and seaworthy cargo-carriers called *knarrs*. Using these fine vessels the Vikings became the first Europeans to make regular transoceanic voyages. However, the first explorers of the North Atlantic were not Vikings, but Irish monks. Consciously placing their fates in the hands of God, monks undertook spiritual voyages, or *peregrinatio*, in search of ultimate solitude. This they found in the uninhabited Faroe Islands, which they had reached by the early seventh century, and in Iceland, which they called Thule, where later Viking settlers claimed to have found crosiers and other ecclesiastical artifacts. Some monks may well have sailed further north to the edge of the Arctic sea-ice but there is no evidence to support claims that they also reached Greenland and North America.

It is not known how the Vikings first learned about the Faroe Islands. Perhaps they were sighted from a ship blown off course on a voyage from Norway to raid or trade in the Scottish islands or Ireland. More likely, the Vikings first heard about the islands from the Irish themselves. In any case, around 825 an Irish monk called Dicuil complained that Vikings had recently arrived in the Faroes causing the few monks and hermits who were living there to flee. The Faroes are spectacularly mountainous islands, windswept and devoid of trees but they have a mild climate for their latitude and grass grows well. As Viking age Scandinavians lived primarily by pastoralism, the islands were therefore an attractive place to settle despite their bleakness. Traditionally the first settler was Grímur Kamban. As his surname is Gaelic in origin, Grímur must have spent some time in Ireland or the Hebrides before settling in the Faroes, but most of the settlers came direct from the Norwegian west-coast districts of Agder, Rogaland and Sogn.

The settlement of the Faroes was simply the prelude to a series of voyages and migrations which

ultimately took the Vikings right across the Atlantic
to become the first Europeans to set foot in the New
World. Around 860 Gardar, a Swedish navigator, was
blown off course during a voyage from Norway to
the Hebrides and eventually sighted an unknown
and uninhabited land which he named Gardarsholm
('Gardar's island') after himself. After a year spent
exploring the entire coastline, Gardar returned to
Norway where, presumably, he had been given up
for lost. Shortly afterwards the new land received
another accidental visitor, Nadodd, who was blown
off course en route from Norway to settle in the
Faroe Islands. Nadodd climbed a mountain, had a
quick look around and seeing no signs of habitation
left in the middle of a blizzard, on account of which
he called his discovery Snowland. Reports of these
voyages inspired Floki Vilgerdarson of Rogaland to
attempt a settlement. Floki was certainly not one of
history's most efficient pioneers. By neglecting to
gather sufficient hay in the summer, his livestock
died during the winter. Floki decided to give up the
settlement as a bad job but heavy drift ice prevented
his escape and he had to spend a second, difficult
winter on the island. Thoroughly disillusioned by
the time he returned home, Floki called the island

Iceland and the name has stuck. Other members of Floki's party, however, gave favourable accounts of the island's good grazing and extensive birch woodlands and by 870 settlers had begun to arrive in large numbers. Even Floki himself returned to settle, successfully this time. In all, the settlement period lasted until about 930 by which time all the best grazing land had been claimed. Except in the broad dales of the south-west, most of the settlements were close to the sea. The barren glaciated mountains and lava plains of the interior remained uninhabited, as indeed they still are. The settlers soon made a bleak land rather bleaker: by 1100 most of the woodland had been felled and overgrazing by cattle and sheep was turning many areas into virtual deserts.

The Icelanders were intensely proud of their origins. In the early twelfth century the historian Ari Thorgilsson drew on a wealth of orally transmitted family histories to compile the *Landnámabók* ('The Book of the Settlements'). This gives the names of some 430 leaders of the settlement period, together with those of many of their followers, the names and locations of their farms and landholdings and, in several cases, their lands of origin. Most of the

69

leaders were men of aristocratic origin who brought with them their families, personal retinues and slaves. They took personal possession of the land, farmed some themselves and on the rest settled their followers as tenants. By far the majority of the settlers whose origins are known came from western Norway but with a significant number coming from southern Norway, the Norse colonies in Ireland and Scotland as well as a few from Denmark and Sweden. Some freed Irish or Scottish slaves were also given farms by their owners and founded families. Several of the settlers who had been living in Scotland and Ireland were Christians but the religion soon died out in Iceland.

According to later Icelandic traditions, the settlement of the Faroe Islands and Iceland was begun by exiles fleeing from the tyrannical rule imposed by King Harald Fairhair of Norway (r. *c.* 880–930) after he united Norway at the battle of Hafrsfjord. Following his victory Harald is said to have claimed all land for the crown, effectively forcing freeholders to become royal tenants. Rather than lose their independence, many preferred to try their luck in the newly discovered lands in the North Atlantic. Attractively simple as this explanation is, it is certainly untrue. Despite considerable uncertainty about the date of the battle of Hafrsfjord, few modern historians believe that it can have taken place much before 885, around fifteen years after the settlements had begun. As Iceland was not fully settled until around 930, Harald's policies may have helped sustain emigration but it cannot have been the initial cause. Despite this, the story does contain an element of truth. The leaders of the settlement were all aristocrats of middle rank – local chieftains – there were no kings or others of royal blood among them as there were among the leaders of the raids on western Europe and no *jarls* ('earls') either. Local chieftains had seen their traditional independence eroded by the growth of royal power in the eighth and ninth centuries so the opportunity to emigrate to a land beyond the reach of kings must have been an attractive one.

The early settlements were lawless, and blood-feuds ran out of control. Local leadership was assumed by the *goðar*, wealthy chieftains who could offer advocacy and protection to smaller landowners in return for their political and military support. The *goðar* presided over the district *things*, the

71

assemblies of freemen at which local disputes and criminal cases were judged. But the district things proved inadequate for resolving major disputes which went beyond the immediate locality and around 930 an annual all-Iceland assembly, the *Althing*, was set up at Thingvellir in the south-west. Iceland was divided into four quarters, corresponding to the points of the compass, which had equal voting rights at the *Althing*. Though all free men could attend, the *Althing* was essentially an oligarchical government, entirely controlled by the thirty-six *goðar* who alone had the right to vote. Despite this, decision making at the *Althing* tended to be consensual. The *goðar* could not take the allegiance of their *thingmen* (supporters) for granted: as freemen they could transfer their support to another chief if their opinions were not taken into account. The only government office was that of the lawspeaker, whose role was to conduct the opening formalities of the *Althing* and recite the orally transmitted laws of Iceland. Though this was an influential office, it carried no executive authority.

For so long as the *goðar* were all of roughly equal wealth and power, the Althing provided Iceland with good government. Perhaps its greatest achievement was the peaceful establishment of Christianity as the official religion in 1000. However, the emergence of a small group of pre-eminent chieftains (known as *storgoðar*, 'great chieftains') in the thirteenth century led to power struggles and civil war as they fought each other for supremacy. In desperation the Icelanders appealed to King Håkon IV of Norway to take over the country and restore order in 1263. In the end, there was no escaping the forces of political centralization. By this time Iceland had other problems. Its lack of good timber meant that once the ships used by the original colonists had rotted, replacements could only be obtained at great expense from abroad; inevitably the island's trade passed under the control of foreigners. Major eruptions from Iceland's many volcanoes had also damaged the agricultural economy and the population began to decline from the peak it had reached around 1100 of about 40,000.

Though in clear weather the high, glaciated island of Greenland can be seen from the mountains of western Iceland, the first European known to have sighted it was Gunnbjorn Ulf-Krakuson, who was blown off course on a voyage from Norway to

Iceland sometime around 900 to 930. Around 978 Snæbjorn Galti tried to settle on some offshore islands discovered by Gunnbjorn but the attempt ended in disaster after a terrible winter. All Gunnbjorn and Snæbjorn had seen was Greenland's heavily glaciated east coast but a few years later Erik the Red, in search of a safe place to spend his exile for manslaughter, rounded Cape Farewell and discovered its ice-free western fjords. By this time all the best land in Iceland had long since been claimed and many latecomers, like Erik himself, were living on very marginal land. The western fjords had good grazing and Erik, who gave Greenland its attractive name, had little difficulty persuading other Icelanders to join him in founding two settlements there in 986: the main Eastern Settlement and the smaller Western Settlement, 300 miles north-west. Later a small settlement grew up between the two. Erik became the acknowledged leader of the settlements, probably taking a role akin to that of the Icelandic lawspeaker.

At first the settlements prospered and the total population reached about 4,000 in the twelfth century. The climate was milder than it is today and it even proved possible to grow a little grain in sheltered places. Cattle and sheep rearing were the basis of the economy but the settlement also exported valuable luxuries such as walrus ivory, polar-bear furs and falcons, taken in the Nordsetr, the rich hunting grounds around Disko Island, north of the Arctic Circle. Some Norse Greenlanders sailed as far as 79° N to trade with the Thule Eskimo people of Ellesmere Island in the Canadian Arctic. The Greenland colony's fortunes went into decline in the thirteenth century. Like the Icelanders, the Greenlanders could not replace their ships, so they increasingly relied on foreigners for their trade and communications with the outside world. Eventually, in 1263, the Greenlanders accepted Norwegian rule in return for trade guarantees. Decline continued in the fourteenth century as the climatic deterioration known as the 'Little Ice Age' set in. Stock rearing suffered and the colonies became increasingly isolated from the outside world by sea-ice. As the climate deteriorated the Thule Eskimo, who were much better adapted to life in the Arctic than the Greenlanders, began to migrate south, encroaching on the settlements. By 1410, when the last recorded ship visited the colony, only the Eastern Settlement still survived. Some contacts with Europe continued after this – clothes preserved in the frozen soil of a cemetery show that the Greenlanders kept up to date with fifteenth-century fashions – but a ship visiting the Eastern Settlement in 1540 found only deserted farms and in one of them a single unburied skeleton, perhaps that of the last lonely survivor of the colony.

The reasons for the extinction of the Greenland colony are unknown. Most commonly cited is the failure of the Greenlanders' agricultural economy due to the climatic deterioration and skeletons excavated from fifteenth-century cemeteries show them to have had health problems specifically related to poor nutrition and declining life expectancy. Conflict with the Eskimos may also have been a factor. Both Icelandic annals and Eskimo folktales record violent clashes between the two peoples, but there are also stories of cooperation and friendship.

The final pulse of the Viking movement west took them to North America. Once again this was an accidental discovery. Around 985 Bjarni Herjolfsson, an Icelandic merchant, was blown off course to a low-lying forested land while sailing to Greenland. Sailing north he encountered a rocky, mountainous, glaciated land before turning east and making a landfall in Greenland. Bjarni was criticized for his lack of curiosity – he had not landed to explore – and fifteen years later Leif Eriksson (Erik the Red's son) set off to retrace his route. Leif first reached the rocky, glaciated land which he called Helluland ('Slab-land'). Most probably this was Baffin Island. Sailing south he reached the forested land, naming it Markland ('Forest-land'). This was probably the coast of Labrador. Leif continued to sail south into completely unknown territory and before returning home spent a winter in a land with a mild climate where grapes grew wild and the rivers teemed with salmon. Leif called this Vinland ('Vine-land'): from its description it must have been somewhere between the Gulf of St Lawrence and Cape Cod. Follow-up voyages were made by other Greenlanders but attempts to settle failed because of the vast distances that had to be covered and the understandable hostility of the native Indians – the Vikings had killed the first ones they had met in an apparently unprovoked attack. Successful European settlement in the Americas had to wait another 500 years. Historians were highly sceptical about the truth of the saga accounts of these voyages until the discovery of a Viking settlement at L'Anse-aux-Meadows in Newfoundland in the 1960s provided dramatic confirmation. During the excavations the discovery of butternuts (a kind of walnut), which do not grow north of the St Lawrence, and evidence of ironworking and ship repair suggests that the settlement was a base for voyages further south, perhaps to Vinland.

The main historical importance of the Vikings' North Atlantic adventure lies not in the discovery of North America but in the settlement of Iceland and the Faroe Islands. These were the only permanent extensions to the Scandinavian world to result from the Viking expansion. Elsewhere in Europe, the Viking settlers were quickly assimilated to the native population, leaving little trace of their presence. In the Faroes and Iceland there was no native population so the settlers retained a Scandinavian identity, rooted in the west-coast districts of Norway, from whose dialects the Icelandic and Faroese languages have evolved. The Icelanders in particular remained proud of their origins and alone of all the Germanic peoples they preserved and recorded the pagan myths and traditions of their ancestors after the conversion to Christianity.

Their abiding interest in family history inspired the magnificent Icelandic sagas, the best of which, such as *Njal's Saga*, rank among the greatest works of world literature and are still widely read and enjoyed today.

SEVEN

East to Russia

Viking activity east of the Baltic was just as enterprising as that in western Europe and the Atlantic but much less is known about it. Apart from short commemorative inscriptions in runes, the Vikings themselves left no contemporary written records and the region was far beyond the horizons of most western European chroniclers. The native Slavs did not use any form of writing until the tenth century (the Balts and Finns even later) and their earliest historical records date to the twelfth. Greeks and Arabs who had direct dealings with Vikings in the east have left the most important accounts. Because of their geographical proximity, it was the Swedes who took the lead in this movement but the Danes were active raiders and traders in the Baltic Sea and we know of several Norwegians and Icelanders who travelled in the east.

In fact, Scandinavian expansion east of the Baltic began long before the beginning of Viking raiding in western Europe. Cemeteries containing Scandinavian merchant graves at the east Baltic trading centres of Grobin in Latvia and Elblag, Poland, show that the earliest phase of expansion began as early as about 650. Grave goods from these cemeteries show that most of these merchants were from central Sweden and the island of Gotland. About 100 years later Scandinavian merchants were established at the then Finnish settlement of Staraja Ladoga, on the River Volkhov in north-east Russia, within easy reach of the Baltic Sea. Connections with the Muslim world were established not long afterwards: one hoard of Arab coins at Staraja Ladoga dates from as early as the 780s. Russia's many navigable rivers made the establishment of long-distance trade routes relatively easy and by the 830s at the latest the Scandinavians had established direct contact with Arab merchants on the Volga and the Greeks at the Byzantine capital, Constantinople (Istanbul). Some enterprising Viking traders even made it all the way to Baghdad, then the largest, richest and most sophisticated city in the world. A large number of female Scandinavian graves have been discovered in Russia, indicating that some

81

of these merchants travelled in family groups. Vast amounts of Arab silver, received in exchange for furs and slaves, began to find its way back to Sweden, where the fate of most of it was to be melted down into ingots to be used either in trade or for making jewelry. Nevertheless many tens of thousands of Arab coins have been discovered in Viking silver hoards which for one reason or another were never recovered by their owners. The Russian trade routes flourished until the exhaustion of the Islamic world's silver mines between 965 and 1015 caused their decline and eventual abandonment. An attempt by Ingvar the Widefarer in about 1041 to reopen the trade routes ended in disaster somewhere in the east: central Sweden is peppered with runic memorial stones to men who died with Ingvar on the expedition. It should not be assumed that because Scandinavian expansion in the east was motivated by trade that it was any less violent than that in the west – far from it. The Scandinavians took over Slav or Finnish settlements, such as Staraja Ladoga, Novgorod and Kiev, and used them as bases from which to raid the neighbouring tribes to force them to pay tribute in furs, slaves and other products such as wax and honey, which could be sold to the Arabs, Greeks or western Europeans. Scandinavian merchants also needed to be ready to defend themselves from ambush by the Slavs or roaming nomad bands. The merchants were particularly vulnerable at portages, places where they had to carry their ships overland from one river system to another or to avoid unnavigable rapids.

Very early on, Scandinavians settled in the east came to be known as the Rus, from which Russia gets its name. The word Rus is most commonly explained as a derivative of *Ruotsi*, the Finnish name for the Swedes during the Viking age. *Ruotsi* itself probably derives from the Scandinavian term *roðr*, meaning a crew of oarsmen. A less widely accepted alternative is that the term is derived from Rosomones (*rusiui* or 'blondes'), the Greek name for the Heruls, a tribe from Jutland who were active in the eastern Roman Empire as pirates and mercenaries between the third and sixth centuries. In the nineteenth and twentieth centuries, and especially during the Soviet period, many Russian historians were unwilling to accept that Scandinavians had played an important role in early Russian history and argued instead that the Rus were really a Slavic people. Although the Rus were eventually completely assimilated to the native Slavs, the evidence for their Scandinavian origins is so strong that it really leaves little room for doubt. Archaeological evidence for Scandinavian settlement in Russia during the Viking age, such as graves furnished with typical Scandinavian artifacts, is plentiful. The Arab writer and traveller Ibn Fadlan has also left us a vivid eyewitness account of the funeral of a Rus chief which involved cremation in a boat with a sacrificed slave girl. This was a Scandinavian rather than a Slavic practice. Contemporary written sources also explicitly confirm the original Scandinavian identity of the Rus. The *Annals of St Bertin* describe the visit of a group of men described as 'Rhos' to the court of the Frankish emperor Louis the Pious as part of a Byzantine delegation in 839. Enquiries by the emperor's agents revealed that they 'belonged to the people of the Swedes'. Louis feared they might be Viking spies. An Italian churchman and diplomat, Liudprand of Cremona, identified Rus pirates who attacked Constantinople in 941 as *nordmanni* ('Northmen'). Similarly, Liudprand's Arab contemporary, the well-travelled writer al-Ya'qubi, identified the Vikings who captured Seville in 844 with 'the pagans who are called *ar-Rus*'. It is also clear that the Rus spoke a Scandinavian language. In his treatise on government, *De administrando imperio*, the Byzantine emperor Constantine VII Porphyrogenitos (r. 913–59) gives both the Rus and Slavic names for the rapids on the river Dnieper: the Rus names (e.g. *Baruforos*, 'Wave-force') are Old Norse. Finally, the names of the earliest rulers of the Rus state – Rurik (Roric), Oleg (Helgi), Olga (Helga) and Igor (Ingvar) – are also of Scandinavian rather than Slavic origin. From the mid-tenth century, Scandinavians were sometimes called 'Varangians' by the Greeks, Arabs and Slavs. Sometimes the term is used interchangeably with 'Rus' but it is more often reserved for Scandinavian merchants and mercenaries newly arrived in the east from their homelands. Today the term is generally used more narrowly to describe members of the Byzantine emperor's elite bodyguard, the Varangian guard, which was recruited from Viking mercenaries. The word Varangian is probably derived from Old Norse *vár*, 'pledge', possibly because bands of Scandinavian merchants and warriors customarily formed sworn fellowships.

By the early tenth century, the Rus had created a powerful state which controlled a vast region stretching from its capital at Kiev north to the Baltic. According to the twelfth-century *Russian Primary Chronicle*, the Slavs were weary of constant internecine warfare so around 860 to 862 they appealed to the Rus to provide them with leaders who would introduce the rule of law. Three brothers came forward: the eldest, Rurik, established himself as the ruler of Novgorod; the second brother, Sineus, was established at Beloozero; and the third, Truvor, at Izborsk. When Rurik's brothers died two years later, he became the ruler of all north-west Russia. Rurik died in about 879 and was succeeded by his kinsman Oleg who captured Kiev from two rival Viking warlords around 882 and made it the capital of the Rus state. Oleg was a great warrior, campaigning against the Slavs, supposedly even attacking Constantinople in 907 and probably leading raids on the Muslim lands around the Caspian Sea. Having been told by a soothsayer that his favourite horse would cause his death, Oleg vowed never to ride it or even look at it again. Five years later the horse died, but when Oleg went to see its skeleton, to mock the soothsayer, he was fatally bitten by a snake which crawled out from among its bones. How much truth there is in these stories it is impossible to say. For example, Byzantine historians failed to notice Oleg's attack on their capital city, and it is more likely that he died in battle than from a snake bite, as Arab sources record the death of an unnamed Rus ruler in battle with the Khazars on the Volga in 913, the traditional year of his death. Most modern historians believe that the *Primary Chronicle* was written mainly to establish the legitimacy of the ruling Kievan dynasty of twelfth-century Russia and consider Rurik and Oleg to be at best semi-legendary characters who were introduced into the story to add to the dynasty's prestige. The first truly historical ruler of the Rus was Igor (r. 913–45), who was traditionally, but improbably, regarded as the son of Rurik. Igor led the unsuccessful attack on Constantinople in 941 and was killed on a tribute-gathering raid against the Slavs – a sign of the predatory nature of the early Rus state – leaving only a young son, Svyatoslav (r. 945–72). The state was held together by the boy's redoubtable mother, Olga, until he came of age. Svyatoslav grew up to become a great war leader. In campaigns against the Khazars and Bulgars he doubled the size of the Kievan realm, but his ambitions alarmed the Byzantines, who defeated him in an epic battle at Pereyeslavets on the River Danube in 971. While returning home the following spring Svyatoslav was ambushed and killed by Pecheneg nomads at the Dneiper rapids, and his vast conquests were quickly lost. The Pechenegs are said to have made his skull into that essential barbarian dinner party accessory, a drinking cup.

Though the Scandinavian presence in Russia is well attested by archaeological finds it is clear from the evidence of Viking cemeteries that the Rus were a minority among a Slavic population even in the towns. In the countryside there is almost no evidence at all of Scandinavian settlement. The Rus must therefore have been a warrior and merchant elite. Although memorial inscriptions on rune stones in Sweden attest that Scandinavian immigration continued into the eleventh century, there are clear signs that by Svyatoslav's time the Rus were becoming assimilated to the Slav majority with whom they intermarried and allied. In 907 and 911 the Rus of Kiev agreed trade treaties with the Byzantine empire: the names of the signatories have survived and they are all Scandinavian. When Igor agreed a new treaty with the Byzantines in 945 nearly half the names are Slavic. Even the ruling dynasty was adopting Slavic names by this time: Igor was the last Rus ruler to have a Scandinavian name. Scandinavian religious beliefs were also fading. Svyatoslav's son Vladimir I (r. 978–1015) worshipped the Slavic thunder god Perun before his conversion to Greek Orthodox Christianity in 988. By then most of the ruling elite must have been Slavic speakers because Slavic became the language of the Church. By the time Kiev reached the height of its power in the reign of Jaroslav the Wise (r. 1019–54), the Rus were entirely Slavic in character. Jaroslav continued to welcome Scandinavian mercenaries and exiles to his court and retained close dynastic ties to Scandinavia – for example, one of his daughters was married to the Norwegian king Harald Hardrada – but these ties were probably no more important to him than those he forged with other European rulers.

Ultimately, the Viking contribution to the development of Russian civilization was small. The Slavic peoples of eastern Europe were at a similar level of social and technological development to the Vikings and they had little to learn from them. A sign of this is that there are only half a dozen Scandinavian loan words in the Russian language.

Many of the Slavs' fortified settlements were developing into true towns but there can be no doubt that the arrival of Scandinavian merchants gave the process enormous impetus, turning small settlements like Novgorod into flourishing cities in less than a century. The most important outside influence on the cultural development of early Russia was in fact Byzantium, a consequence of Vladimir I's decision to convert to Orthodox rather than Roman Christianity. Kievan Russia's alphabet, architecture, art, law, music and political ideologies were all essentially Byzantine in origin.

EIGHT

The Scandinavian Kingdoms

The story of the Vikings began with political developments inside Scandinavia and it also ends with them. The main factor in the outbreak of Viking raiding was the centralization of power within Scandinavia itself. This process continued, often violently, throughout the ninth and tenth centuries until in the eleventh century Denmark and Norway had emerged as stable territorial kingdoms – Sweden took a little longer. An important element in the completion of this process was conversion to Christianity, which opened Scandinavia to powerful European cultural influences. Christian missions to Scandinavia had begun early in the eighth century but the religion had little impact until the late tenth century, when it began to win royal converts, who often used harsh measures to persuade their subjects to convert too. Scandinavian kings, while no doubt sincere converts, were not blind to the potential of Christianity as a unifying force and of the doctrine of divinely ordained kingship which placed the king far above his subjects. The Church also had literate personnel to help the king to build effective governmental institutions. With the consolidation of royal power, kings came increasingly to rely on institutionalized means of wealth gathering, such as taxation and tolls, and there was no longer the same pressure to lead hazardous plundering raids abroad. Kings frowned upon freelance Viking piracy as a threat to trade and good relations with neighbouring kingdoms and it was gradually suppressed. In any case, for the ambitious there was now the prospect of careers in royal service and the Church, while the crusading movement, which began in 1096, offered a route to glory for the martially inclined. Viking raiding did not come to a sudden end, but by 1100 it had all but died out except in areas where central authority was weak, such as the Scottish islands.

The most advanced of the Scandinavian kingdoms in the Viking era was Denmark. By around 800 the Danes had already created a kingdom which included most of modern Denmark, parts of southern Sweden and Norway and northern Germany. The Danish king at this time, Godfred (d. 810), was much preoccupied by the potential threat of the mighty Carolingian empire which under Charlemagne had extended its sway to the neck of the Jutland peninsula. There is no evidence that Charlemagne ever contemplated invading Denmark but Godfred could not be sure and he pursued an aggressive policy towards the Franks and their Slav allies. After Godfred was murdered in 810 a complex struggle for the throne broke out within the royal family which saw various factions retreat into exile to lick their wounds, seek foreign support or go raiding until they had gathered enough strength to return and try their luck again. The issue was not completely resolved until 827, when Horik (r. 813–54), a son of Godfred, emerged as the unchallenged ruler. Great survivor though he was, Horik was eventually killed, along with most of the royal family, in a civil war which was sparked by an ambitious homecoming Viking leader.

After Horik's death Denmark disappeared into obscurity for nearly a century: it was frequently divided and from about 900 to 936 part of the country was ruled by a Swedish dynasty. The Swedes were expelled by Hardegon and soon after his son Gorm founded a new and illustrious dynasty. Gorm's direct authority was probably limited to Jutland; elsewhere in Denmark he exercised power only through the intermediary of local chieftains. It was the achievement of Gorm's son Harald Bluetooth (r. 958–87) to weld Denmark into a unified kingdom by building and garrisoning a series of circular forts so that he could exercise direct authority throughout the kingdom. Harald also reasserted Danish power in Norway. In 965 Harald was converted to Christianity by Poppo, a German missionary, an event he commemorated with an impressive runic stone at Jelling in Jutland. He became the first Scandinavian king actively to promote Christianity to his subjects and by 1000 Denmark was largely Christian. Despite his achievements Harald was overthrown by his son Svein Forkbeard (r. 987–1014) and he died in exile. The resurgence of Viking raiding in the late tenth century was a direct threat to Svein's authority. Successful Viking leaders such as Olaf Tryggvason and Thorkell the

Tall began to rival Svein in wealth and reputation. The danger was made all too plain when Olaf used his plunder to finance a successful bid for control of Norway. Svein's response was to bolster his own prestige and wealth by leading his own plundering and tribute-gathering raids on England. Svein's raids culminated in the outright conquest of England late in 1013 but he died a few weeks later.

Svein was succeeded in Denmark by his son Harald II and his intention was that another son, Cnut, would inherit England. The English would have none of it, though, and Cnut had to reconquer the country in 1015 to 1016. When his brother died in 1018, Cnut returned to Denmark and was accepted there as king. In 1028 Cnut added Norway to his dominions and around 1030 he was accepted as overlord by the Swedish kings. Recognition of Cnut's stature as a major European ruler came in 1027 when he travelled to Rome to attend the coronation of the Holy Roman Emperor, Henry II. Cnut's achievements boosted Danish prestige but he recognized that England was the most valuable of his possessions and he ruled in Denmark through the intermediary of regents. Cnut failed to give his empire any institutional unity and it broke up on his death. Denmark was even briefly under Norwegian rule until Cnut's nephew Svein Estrithson (r. 1047–74) led a successful rebellion in 1046. Svein had to fight the Norwegian King, Harald Hardrada, for sixteen long years before Danish independence was recognized. Although Svein gave rather half-hearted support to two rebellions against William the Conqueror in England, and his son Cnut II (r. 1080–6) planned a further invasion, by the second half of the eleventh century Danish concerns were increasingly focused on the Baltic Sea. Having adopted Scandinavian shipbuilding methods, the pagan Wends (Slavs) had begun to launch Viking-style raids from their homelands on the southern shore of the Baltic Sea on southern Sweden and the Danish islands. In response the Danes built fortified churches, restored ancient hillforts and blocked harbours and inlets with barriers of stakes driven into the sea bed. Despite this, it was only after their homelands had been conquered by German and Danish crusaders in the early thirteenth century that the Wendish raids ceased.

At the beginning of the Viking age Norway was still divided into many small kingdoms and chiefdoms and part of the south was under Danish control. The Danes lost control of the south during the ninth century and around 885 to 890, Harald Finehair (r. *c.* 880–930), the king of Vestfold southwest of Oslo Fjord, succeeded in bringing most of Norway under his control at the battle of Hafrsfjord. Because of this Harald is traditionally regarded as the founder of the kingdom of Norway but he certainly did not exercise direct rule throughout Norway – the powerful jarl Håkon of Hlaðir (near Trondheim) had named autonomy as the price of his support and there remained several petty kings. The independence of the jarls of Hlaðir was to prove a severe obstacle to the effective unification of Norway. The power of the jarls made them king makers and breakers, and it was a power they did not hesitate to use. They were also understandably reluctant to see the monarchy grow too strong, as it would threaten their independence. For this reason they were often prepared to support the claims of the Danish kings to sovereignty over Norway because they were too far distant to intervene effectively.

Before he died Harald arranged for his kingdom to be divided between his many sons. Harald's favourite, though not eldest, son, Erik Bloodaxe (r. *c.* 930–6) was to be high king over them all. The settlement did not last as the brothers fell out over their inheritance, each believing he had the right to full kingship. Harald's rule was unpopular even before he killed two of his brothers and around 936 he was forced to abdicate by his half-brother Håkon the Good (r. *c.* 936–60), who won the support of jarl Sigurd of Hlaðir. Håkon had been brought up a Christian at the court of king Athelstan in England but he soon abandoned his tentative attempts at evangelization in the face of hostile public opinion. With this experiment behind him Håkon became a popular ruler, but eventually was mortally wounded in battle with Harald Greycloak (r. 960–*c.* 970), a son of Erik Bloodaxe, and his Danish allies. Harald was a militant Christian and his attempts at forced evangelization alienated his subjects. When he murdered Sigurd of Hlaðir, Harald drove his son Håkon the Great into the arms of Harald Bluetooth of Denmark, and together they overthrew him. Håkon and Harald Bluetooth divided Norway between them, but Harald had problems on the German border and within a few years jarl Håkon had become effectively the ruler of all of Norway.

Håkon was himself overthrown in 995 by Olaf Tryggvason, the son of a minor Norwegian king (murdered by Harald Greycloak) who had made a fortune and earned a great reputation as a warrior by leading Viking raids on England. By overthrowing the jarldom of Hlaðir, Olaf became the first king to exercise direct authority throughout Norway. While in England, Olaf had converted to Christianity and he was determined that his subjects should do so too. Opposition was ruthlessly dealt with and by 1000 most of the coastal districts of Norway were at least nominally Christian. Olaf also persuaded the Icelanders to accept Christianity as their official religion. However, neither Svein nor jarl Håkon's exiled son Erik were reconciled to their loss of influence in Norway. Together, in 1000, they ambushed Olaf's fleet at the battle of Svöld. His forces defeated, Olaf jumped over the side of his flagship and sank without a trace. Svein and jarl Erik now divided Norway between them, but Olaf's achievement was not forgotten. When jarl Erik left to support Cnut's invasion of England in 1015 Olaf Haraldsson, another royal exile turned Viking, invaded Norway and claimed the throne. Olaf completed the Christianization of Norway, though the brutal methods he used caused widespread discontent. The local chieftains also felt threatened by Olaf's measures to strengthen royal authority and, hoping for a return to the days of weak indirect Danish rule, in 1028 they allied with Cnut and chased their king into exile. Olaf attempted to win back his kingdom in 1030 but was defeated and killed by a peasant army at the battle of Stiklestad. Miracles were soon reported at Olaf's burial place and he was later recognized as Norway's national saint.

Cnut appointed his son Svein King of Norway under the regency of the boy's mother, Ælfgifu, an English concubine. Ælfgifu made herself enormously unpopular by her efforts to further centralize royal power, and around the time of Cnut's death in 1035, St Olaf's son Magnus the Good (r. 1035–47) returned from exile and drove her and Svein out of Norway. Reversing the normal order of things, Magnus also became King of Denmark in 1042.

Magnus' successor, his uncle Harald Hardrada (r. 1046–66), is generally recognized as the last great Viking leader. Harald's career began when he fought for his half-brother St Olaf at Stiklestad aged fifteen. Harald went into exile in the east, serving as a mercenary in the army of prince Jaroslav of Novgorod-Kiev and in the Byzantine emperor's Varangian guard at Constantinople. Having made himself rich and famous, Harald returned to Norway and was accepted as joint king by Magnus in 1046, becoming sole king on Magnus' death a year later. Harald embarked on his fruitless struggle with Svein Estrithson but finally had to accept Danish independence in 1064. Harald was not a popular ruler in Norway and the ruthless means he used to defend his authority earned him his nickname *harðráði* ('hard ruler'). Following the death of King Edward the Confessor in 1066, Harald invaded England to claim the throne, only to be killed at the battle of Stamford Bridge. Casualties were so heavy that it was a generation before a Norwegian King was again able to embark on an overseas expedition.

Sweden is the Scandinavian kingdom we know least about in the Viking age. The relationship between the Svear and Götar, the two main peoples of Viking Sweden, was already close at the beginning of the Viking era. Some kings of the Götar, such as Alrik who ruled Västergötland in about 800, are known to have been members of the Svear royal family, while some kings of the Svear originated among the Götar. The Götar are not mentioned in contemporary sources as being involved either in Viking raiding in the west or in trading ventures in Russia. Even western Europeans who visited Sweden, such as the missionary St Ansgar, failed to notice them. This is probably more a sign that they were so dominated by the Svear that, to an outsider at least, they were indistinguishable from them, than that they were a race of stay-at-homes. The first king who is known for certain to have ruled both the Svear and the Götar was Olof Skötkonung (r. 995–1022) but this was simply a dynastic union. The two peoples were usually ruled by the same king from Olof's time onwards but they were not permanently united as a single kingdom until 1172. The large and prosperous Baltic island of Gotland was also only gradually drawn into the kingdom of Sweden, entering a tributary arrangement in the eleventh century but not being fully incorporated until the thirteenth. Christianity was slower to become established in Sweden than in the other Scandinavian countries. The religion was first actively promoted in Sweden by Olof Skötkonung, who founded the country's first bishopric at Skara in 1014, but the pagan cult centre at Uppsala was still flourishing at the end of the twelfth century and one king, Blot-Sven (r. 1080–3), even led a brief pagan revival (his nickname comes from *blót*, the Old Scandinavian word for a pagan sacrificial feast). Sweden was not to be fully Christianized until the end of the twelfth century.

By the end of the twelfth century the three Scandinavian kingdoms of Denmark, Norway and Sweden had developed into typical medieval European Christian states: European Romanesque and Gothic art and architecture had replaced traditional Viking styles; the Latin alphabet was replacing the ancient Germanic runic alphabet; chivalric romances became fashionable as the traditional Viking literary forms such as skaldic verse fell out of favour; and mounted knights had replaced the heavily armed infantryman on the battlefield. Despite some residual internal instability the Scandinavian kingdoms were beginning a period of territorial expansion. The Danes and Swedes were both heavily involved in the crusades against the pagan Wends and Balts of the south and eastern coasts of the Baltic Sea. The Danes would even briefly become the dominant power in the Baltic under Valdemar II (r. 1202–41), though they soon lost their empire to the Germans. The Swedes began the conquest of the Finns in the mid-twelfth century and by the end of the thirteenth century had expanded to the borders of Russia. The large Swedish-speaking minority in Finland is a legacy of this movement. These Swedish and Danish conquests in the east played an important part in spreading the influence of Catholic Christian civilization in eastern Europe. Norway did not have the same opportunities for territorial expansion at the expense of politically less advanced peoples that the Danes and Swedes had, but it did gain control over the Faroe Islands (*c.* 1180), Greenland (1261) and Iceland (1263). The Norwegians also participated in the crusading movement, with major expeditions to the Holy Land being led by King Sigurd Jorsalafari ('Jerusalem-farer') in 1107 and earl Rognvald Kali of Orkney in 1153. The one-time terrors of Christendom had now well and truly joined the ranks of its defenders.

Further Reading

PRIMARY SOURCES IN TRANSLATION

A wide range of primary sources is available in translation.
Among the most enjoyable to read are the Icelandic sagas but it
must be remembered, for all their terse realism and convincing
detail, that they were written over two hundred years after the
events they describe.

Anglo-Saxon Chronicle, trans. N. Garmonsway (London, Dent, 1953).
The most important source for Viking activity in England.
Annals of St Bertin, trans. J.L. Nelson (Manchester University
Press, 1991). Detailed annals covering the majority of the
period of the most intensive Viking raiding on the Continent.
Egil's Saga, trans. H. Pálsson and P. Edwards (Harmondsworth,
Penguin, 1977). One of the most entertaining Icelandic
sagas: its hero Egil is a larger-than-life character whose
adventures take him across much of the Viking world.
King Harald's Saga: Harald Hardradi of Norway, trans. M.
Magnusson and H. Pálsson (Harmondsworth, Penguin,
1966). Biography of the last great Viking leader.

Njal's Saga, trans. M. Magnusson and H. Pálsson (Harmondsworth, Penguin, 1960). Simply the finest of the Icelandic sagas and one of the great works of world literature.

Vinland Sagas, trans. M. Magnusson and H. Pálsson (Harmondsworth, Penguin, 1965). The Norse voyages to Greenland and North America.

Poetic Edda, trans. C. Larrington (Oxford University Press, 1996). A fine translation of pagan Norse mythological poems.

SECONDARY SOURCES

This is a highly selective list, concentrating on recent works which are suitable for the general reader; most of them should be readily available.

Bates, D., *Normandy before 1066* (London, Longman, 1982). An excellent study of the Viking origins and early history of Normandy.

Byock, J.L., *Medieval Iceland: Society, Sagas and Power* (Berkeley, Los Angeles and London, Hisarlik, 1988). Superb analysis of Icelandic society at the end of the Viking age.

Clarke, H. and Ambrosiani, B., *Towns in the Viking Age* (2nd rev. edn, Leicester University Press, 1995). A useful and wide-ranging survey of the archaeology of Viking towns from Ireland to Russia.

Ellis Davidson, H.R., *The Viking Road to Byzantium* (London, George Allen & Unwin, 1976). A well-written account of Viking activities in eastern Europe and beyond.

Foote, P.G. and Wilson, D.M., *The Viking Achievement* (2nd rev. edn, London, Sidgwick & Jackson, 1980). A wide-ranging survey of all aspects of Viking life and culture.

Graham-Campbell, J. (ed.), *Cultural Atlas of the Viking World* (Oxford and New York, Facts on File, 1994). A good introduction to Viking history and culture, though rather short on maps for a historical atlas.

Graham-Campbell, J. and Batey, C.E., *Vikings in Scotland: an Archaeological Survey* (Edinburgh University Press, 1998).

Haywood, J., *The Penguin Historical Atlas of the Vikings* (London, Penguin, 1995).

Haywood, J., *Encyclopedia of the Viking Age* (London, Thames and Hudson, forthcoming). A handy A–Z reference book including brief biographies of the most important figures of the Viking age.

Jochens, J., *Women in Old Norse Society* (Ithaca and London, Cornell University Press, 1995). Surveys all aspects of women's lives in the late Viking age.

Jones, G., *A History of the Vikings* (Oxford University Press, 1968). The best narrative history of the Viking era.

Jones, G., *The Norse Atlantic Saga* (2nd edn, Oxford University Press, 1986). A very readable account of the Vikings' adventures in the North Atlantic.

Logan, F.D., *The Vikings in History* (London, Hutchinson, 1983). It has a particularly good account of the Viking raids on the Continent.

Richards, J.D., *Viking Age England* (London, Batsford, 1991). An introduction to the archaeology of Viking England.

Roesdahl, E., *Viking Age Denmark* (London, British Museum Press, 1982). A detailed study of the archaeology of Viking Denmark.

Roesdahl, E., *The Vikings* (London, Penguin, 1991). A short introductory survey.

Roesdahl, E. and Wilson, D.M. (eds), *From Viking to Crusader: Scandinavia and Europe 800–1200* (Copenhagen, Nordic Council of Ministers, 1992). A wonderfully illustrated exhibition catalogue with many useful supporting articles on aspects of Scandinavian history and culture in the early Middle Ages.

Sawyer, P.H., *The Age of the Vikings* (London, Arnold, 1962). A controversial book which has had an enormous influence on the study of the Viking age.

Sawyer, P.H., *Kings and Vikings* (London, Methuen, 1982). Strong on the causes and consequences of the Viking age.

Sawyer, P.H., (ed.), *The Oxford Illustrated History of the Vikings* (Oxford University Press, 1997). Probably the best introduction to the history of the Viking age currently available.

Wilson, D.M., *The Vikings and their Origins* (3rd rev. edn, London, Thames and Hudson, 1989). A brief, well illustrated study of Viking origins.

Index